Spooky
Creepy
North Dakota

Spooky Creepy North Dakota

Lori L. Orser

4880 Lower Valley Road, Atglen, Pennsylvania 19310

Dedication

This book is dedicated to my parents, Loyd and Marlys Orser, who never stopped believing in me.

Schiffer Books are available at special discounts for bulk purchases for sales promotions or premiums. Special editions, including personalized covers, corporate imprints, and excerpts can be created in large quantities for special needs. For more information contact the publisher:

Published by Schiffer Publishing Ltd.
4880 Lower Valley Road
Atglen, PA 19310
Phone: (610) 593-1777; Fax: (610) 593-2002
E-mail: Info@schifferbooks.com

For the largest selection of fine reference books on this and related subjects,
please visit our web site at **www.schifferbooks.com**
We are always looking for people to write books on new and related subjects.
If you have an idea for a book please contact us at the above address.

This book may be purchased from the publisher.
Include $5.00 for shipping.
Please try your bookstore first.
You may write for a free catalog.

In Europe, Schiffer books are distributed by
Bushwood Books
6 Marksbury Ave.
Kew Gardens
Surrey TW9 4JF England
Phone: 44 (0) 20 8392-8585; Fax: 44 (0) 20 8392-9876
E-mail: info@bushwoodbooks.co.uk
Website: www.bushwoodbooks.co.uk

All photos unless otherwise noted are courtesy of the author

Library of Congress Control Number: 2010930821

Designed by Mark David Bowyer
Type set in Decaying / New Baskerville BT

ISBN: 978-0-7643-3567-9
Printed in the United States of America

Contents

Acknowledgments

A lot of people were involved in the creation of this book, and I want to thank them all. First, writer and mentor Jane Kirkpatrick, who introduced me to Women Writing the West and encouraged me to follow my dreams; Kathleen Ernst, past president of WWW who brought a publisher's call for writers to the group; Susan Tweit, another member of WWW who has provided inspiration and the push to keep on writing;

My sisters, without whom I probably wouldn't still be here: Nancy, who continues to remind me that I'm an author, and that I really can write, and Shari, who encourages me and has been an eagle-eyed first reader; if any errors slipped past her, they're entirely my fault;

Members of Dakota Paranormal Investigators in Fargo, especially founder Nik Guse, who shared with me information from their investigations, photographs, and so much more; members of Night Light Paranormal Investigations in Grand Forks, especially Patty Newark, who worked tirelessly to get me information, and Lorrie Hanson, whose photographs were a godsend;

Wes Anderson of the Barnes County historical society, without whom I wouldn't have known of the early Valley City area spooks and news accounts, and who has encouraged me and helped keep my spirits up; Twilla Glinz of the Bottineau County Historical Society, who told me about some haunted houses; and Doug Ellison, who with his wife Mary owns one of the few remaining independent bookstores in the state, and provided me with the first "true" ghost story to appear in print in Dakota Territory;

Genealogists and researchers extraordinaire, Cynthia Stewart and David A. Holzworth, whose persistent digging – for an entire month – gave a whole new slant to an old murder;

Photographers Mariah Masilko, who let me use her beautiful photos from places I couldn't reach, and Steven Braun, whose author photograph makes me blush;

Authors Michael Norman and Tom Ogden, whose correspondence was both enlightening and encouraging;

Jeani Borchert, for stories of her family and of her work with First Nations peoples;

The staff at the North Dakota State Library and the North Dakota State Archives, for patiently finding obscure reports and newspaper articles, letting me keep books past due dates, and showing me how to use the microfilm reader at least five times without tossing me out, and asking me if I was done yet almost every day!

And to anyone I left out, I apologize; you'll be in the next one.

Introduction

It's true that if you count only the living, North Dakota is one of the least populated states in the country. The mainly agricultural economy of the state leaves wide open spaces, and a traveler driving through the state will see abandoned farmhouses, churches, and in some cases, entire towns. But just because they seem deserted doesn't mean they are. Other presences make their homes here, and they don't plan on leaving any time soon.

Abandoned and cannibalized brick and wood house near Sims church.

Neighbors, former residents, and groups like the Dakota Paranormal Investigators and Night Light Paranormal Investigations will all tell you that spirits of the dead remain in many of the places where, as living people, they lived, worked, played, and died. The descendants of the stolid Germans and Norwegians who make up the majority of the state's population are often reluctant to admit that ghosts exist, but they're quick to tell you where they wouldn't spend a night.

As early as 1883, ghost stories began to appear in newspapers around what was still Dakota Territory. The *Bismarck Weekly Tribune* of August 31, 1883, carried a story of two Bismarck policemen who saw a ghostly woman in white while patrolling downtown one night. The figure walked toward them, then vanished. The article continued with a discussion about a similar sighting a few days previously of a male figure that moved "as silently as a stream of light." Those watching that phantom, including the article's author, started to follow it, hoping to catch a glimpse of its face – only to have it disappear as abruptly as the policemen's female specter. The journalist concluded, "These are no sensational or imaginary yarns, but solid, irrefutable facts."

Twenty years later, in June of 1903, the *Valley City Times-Record* printed an opinion piece with a quite different attitude about "Seeing a Ghost." The writer prescribes a particular manner of squinting if you think you see a ghost. If you see only one outline, rather than two, when using his method, then you are viewing subjectively rather than objectively, and are probably one of the "many nervous and brain-wearied people who see spooks," and should visit a "capable doctor" who can stop you from being haunted by your own imagination.

Less than three months later, in late August of 1903, the Valley City paper returned to the ghostly, again with a cynical attitude. It printed a news article about a haunted barn near Litchville. Over the previous winter the barn's original owner died from coal gas poisoning. The tenant who moved into the farm in the spring left after only a few days. His reason? He claimed that each morning his horses were lathered with sweat, so he decided to move somewhere more restful. Some of the neighbors had reported seeing moving lights around the house at night. The journalist, tongue firmly in cheek, concluded the story by noting that a group of ghost-hunters, headed by his own editor, had gone out to the farmstead one night to check it out, but that "all the spirits they found were brought with them."

Today's ghost stories are more likely to be found on the Internet than in newspapers. A search will bring up pages of website listings, each site filled with a host of haunted, and sometimes haunting, ghost stories from all over the country, and all over the world. There are stories of haunted homes and historic places, creepy hospitals, and terrors lurking in university halls. The only problem is that anyone with a computer can post a ghost story, more or less anonymously, with or without anything to back it up. The trick is determining which stories are valid – that is, which stories have real history behind them and are told by more than one person – and which of them are urban legends, or outright frauds. Stories of all those types are included in this book, and it should be obvious which are which.

So read on. And if you're heading to North Dakota for a vacation, or you live here and believe you live alone, these tales of haunted North Dakota places and spooky monsters might help you stay chilly on the warmest of summer days, and help you add a few destinations to your itinerary.

An abandoned house in eerie Tagus, North Dakota.

Haunted Houses

Stories of haunted houses seem to exist in every town, no matter how big or small. One creepy-looking building, or a run-down home in an otherwise well-maintained neighborhood, is often all it takes to get the stories started.

But some nice-looking houses really are haunted, or at least the people who live in them or visit them believe they are. It's easier to proclaim that a public or well-known home, perhaps a museum or an abandoned house, is haunted, than it is to get a home owner to admit that his or her residence has a ghost. Most people in that situation don't want others to know that they live in a haunted house; perhaps they think others will consider them to be a little "off," or maybe they just don't want the notoriety. But a few are willing to tell their tales. Read on, for both public, abandoned, and private haunted homes.

Former Governor's Mansion, Bismarck

In a residential area just north of Bismarck's downtown business district is a big, beautiful, and remarkably well-preserved late Victorian home. It was built in 1884 by a local businessman, Asa Fisher. He was a very successful businessman, and his house showed it. The home had fifteen rooms, not including the attic or basement, that included five bedrooms, two parlors, porches upstairs and down, and, most grand for its time, an indoor bathroom on the second floor. (A second bathroom was added to the first floor during one of Governor Langer's terms in office.)

Mr. Fisher sold his mansion to the state in 1893, to be used as the governor's residence. Twenty North Dakota governors lived there, beginning with Governor Eli C.D. Shortridge in 1893 and ending with John E. Davis, who left office in 1960. That year a new executive residence was built on the State Capitol Grounds for use by future governors.

The mansion served as offices for several years after 1960, until the State Historical Society of North Dakota (SHSND) took possession in 1975 and began the long and often frustrating process of restoring it to the way it appeared in 1893, to the point of having custom wallpaper made to match original wallpaper discovered by removing multiple layers of the stuff. With justifiable pride, the SHSND has highlighted features of the restoration, including samples of more than 75 different wallpapers that were discovered during the work in the house.

During the many years the building housed governors, only one governor, Frank A. Briggs, died in office, on August 9, 1898. Nothing strange or unusual was noticed in the mansion over the next few years, until Governor John Burke and his family moved in, in early 1907. The Burkes built a finished playroom in the attic for their children, and another part of the attic was the living quarters for Tom Lee, who served as both cook and butler to the Burke family.

Whether Lee heard that Governor Briggs had died in the home and assumed that his spirit must haunt the building, or whether he actually experienced paranormal activity in the mansion isn't on the record. What is certain is that he insisted the house was haunted by Briggs and refused to stay in it alone. When the Burkes were away, Tom Lee slept in a hammock on the second floor porch rather than inside, in his attic room.

Former Governor's Mansion in Bismarck.

Off and on since then, there have been whispered rumors of paranormal activity: a cold spot in the maids rooms (possibly because the only heat source there for years was one register over the kitchen floor), unexplained footsteps on the stairs to the attic and the basement as well as those between the first and second floors, and footsteps in the attic when no one was there. Most of the rumored activity focuses on the master bedroom where Briggs died. The door is said to open and close when no one is there; curtains move when there's no breeze; the closet door slams shut by itself.

No employees of the SHSND are willing to use their own names and say that they have heard or seen anything out of the ordinary. To a person, they all say that an unnamed someone else, or someone's friend, told them something in confidence, though many are quick to tell stories.

So, is the Former Governor's Mansion haunted, or not? I got one clue when I was walking through the building. I was the only visitor for most of the time I was there, and was making notes to myself on a small digital voice recorder. At one point I stood outside the stairs to the attic, which was roped off, and said, "They must not want anyone to go up there." Later, when going through my notes, I heard a whisper right after that, saying what sounded like "Don't go up!" I was astonished; I'm not a paranormal investigator, and the last thing I expected was an EVP (electronic voice phenomenon; not heard when making the recording, but heard when the recording is played, and considered paranormal). But there it was. And no one else was even on the second floor at the time.

If you want an experience of your own, you'll have to go visit the mansion, located on the corner of 4th Street and Avenue B. Admission is free, and it's open from 1 to 5 p.m., Wednesdays through Sundays, between May 16th and September 15th. Halloween events are sometimes held on October 31st; check with the SHSND before you go.

Custer House
Fort Abraham Lincoln, South of Mandan

The Custer House at Fort Abraham Lincoln, 7 miles south of Mandan on Highway 1806, and near the Heart River, isn't the original house that Col. George A. Custer and his wife, Elizabeth (Libbie) moved into in 1873. It isn't even the house that was rebuilt after the first one basically burned to the ground in the winter of 1874. No, it was rebuilt during the 1980s and 1990s using the plans of the 1874 house. It has as many

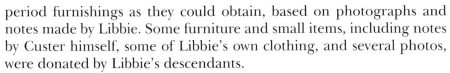

period furnishings as they could obtain, based on photographs and notes made by Libbie. Some furniture and small items, including notes by Custer himself, some of Libbie's own clothing, and several photos, were donated by Libbie's descendants.

The location of the house is the original site, and is now part of Ft. Abraham Lincoln State Park, which includes Ft. Lincoln, a cavalry post built in 1873 to supplement the infantry post stationed there in 1872 to protect the workers building the railroad, the hill-top blockhouses, rebuilt by the Civilian Conservation Corps in the 1930s, that were used by the infantry, and some rebuilt earth lodges from the Mandan Indians' On-A-Slant village, which was abandoned before Lewis and Clark made their journey up the Missouri. The land was donated to the state by President Theodore Roosevelt in 1907.

The house was quite magnificent for that time and place; all the furnishings, and even the windows, had to be carried by train from places like Chicago and New York. But Libbie Custer was determined to have a civilized home, and to entertain the officers' wives just as she had always done. Col. Custer, of course, felt that they deserved no less. His brother, Lt. Tom Custer, was also stationed at the fort, and was a frequent dinner guest. The Custers had three servants, a black woman named Mary, who was primarily their cook, and her two sisters. Mary didn't appreciate Tom's penchant for bringing home wild animals of the prairie, like a baby cougar cub that grew far too quickly, and inhabited the basement where many of her cooking supplies were stored.

If you visit the Fort, and you step across a marked line onto the boardwalk, the year is 1875 – to you. Your first guide will be in an authentic 7th Cavalry uniform – blue wool trousers and jacket, unbelievably hot and scratchy in the North Dakota summer heat. Once you reach the Custer House, your guide may stay with you, or he may hand you off to a woman dressed in the clothing of a maid or laundress of the period. They'll take you through the house and tell you about the furnishings, and what living on the prairie – a wilderness in 1875 – was like. There are his and hers outhouses in back of the Custer house, and you can still see some of the original foundation stones of the officers quarters. Those buildings, along with the barracks, the commissary, and the stables, were cannibalized for building materials when the fort was abandoned in 1881. Its importance had faded as the railroad was built and the Indians were forced onto reservations.

But if you ask the right people, you'll find that the house isn't in 1875 for everyone. If you remember history, you'll know that on June 25th, 1876, the Battle of the Little Big Horn took place. All of the Seventh

Cavalry who had left the fort, heading west with such confidence in early June, were dead. Libbie, as she did most days, had the other officers' wives with her at her home that afternoon, and recorded that she and the other wives were struck that day by a deep sorrow, a feeling of impending doom. The day that word was brought, the wives were again all at the Custer home, so they all heard together. Imagine, if you can, the grief of these suddenly widowed women, knowing how their husbands had been killed, and fearing for their futures and those of their children. So many men gone. Libbie wore black for the rest of her life, it's said. And some say that she and the other officers' wives still remain in the Custer House, trapped in their sorrow from 1876.

One of the assistant supervisors is said to have arrived at the park one morning and found that the motion detector alarm inside the Custer House had gone off during the night. He hurried to the house and found all the doors securely locked, and all the windows locked from the inside. Once he unlocked the doors and turned off the motion detector, he searched the house to find what had caused the detector to go off. He found nothing. Another park employee, going to open up the Custer House early on another morning, decided to go in through the back door. As he approached the house, he looked up and saw a woman's figure in black at one of the windows. Somewhat alarmed, he unlocked the door and went upstairs immediately. There was no one in the room where he'd seen the figure, or indeed in any other part of the house. That morning the motion detector hadn't gone off. Both of these employees are higher-ups, and not the over-imaginative type; if they say they saw something, you can believe it.

In 2006, Bismarck's KXMB TV reporter Julie Cronin paid a visit to the Custer House and spoke with Tracy Potter of the Ft. Lincoln Foundation, the organization that helps fund the Park and oversees the operations. Mr. Potter stated that some people have claimed to see a woman's face looking out of the back window at them, when no one was inside the building. The young summer employees, the "kids" as he calls them, often feel like they're being watched if they're working late at night (the Park has an evening melodrama performance throughout much of the summer). Sometimes the bed in the upstairs bedroom, neatly made for one group, will show the clear imprint of a body when the next tour comes through. And the kids say that things they put away at night in the house are rearranged the next morning, or completely out of place.

The Custer House at Ft. Abraham Lincoln State Park, Mandan.

Visitors who've heard the stories come prepared to feel something eerie in the Custer House, but at times, according to Mr. Potter, even visitors who haven't heard them have seen and felt that something was there, although it wasn't visible to them. Movements or images are sometimes seen as just a flash, and then they're gone.

Potter recounted for Ms. Cronin that one night, he, the Foundation's director, and another friend decided to check the house out for themselves. They played pool in the upstairs game room, but the balls wouldn't go where they were being shot. They seemed to "bend" strangely. Then the group heard the sound of thunder outside – always a possibility after a hot summer day on the prairie – and decided to head for home before the storm really struck. But when they got outside, there was no trace of clouds; the sky was clear and starry. Was the pool table just old and uneven? Do staff see what they expect to see?

In August of 2009, Dakota Paranormal Investigators (DPI) held an investigation at Fort Abraham Lincoln. They started well after dark, when the Custer House and other Park Buildings were closed to visitors. First, a tour guide led them through the house, pointing out the various items, including those donated by Libbie Custer's family, as well as the other features of the house, and during that tour they had both audio and video equipment turned on. Then the tour guide left them to set up their equipment.

Nothing much happened at the house, at least that they could see or hear. However, when they went through the tapes later, and they reached the point where the tour guide was telling them what things had belonged to the Custers, an EVP is clear on the recording, saying "and the pictures" as if to remind the guide that those, too, belonged to Libbie and George. Later in the evening, another quite eerie EVP says clearly, "more of the men have been dying."

Other things happened at other buildings in the fort that night. A medium accompanying the group who was investigating the stables said she saw the spirit of a man holding the picture of a woman; she said that the man had married shortly before the Cavalry was set to leave for Montana Territory, only to find out that his wife was a man. He hanged himself in the stable rather than face the humiliation of the situation. Her statements haven't yet been researched historically, so that information isn't verified. The group investigating the barracks building had a rather long conversation with something that lit up the K-2 meter (an electromagnetic field detector) in answer to questions. Then they asked the entity if it wanted them to leave. Although they heard nothing at the time, the tape revealed an EVP saying "please leave" right after the question was asked.

Perhaps the most exciting evidence they caught was when one group, between the barracks and the commissary, saw a figure walking past each of the windows in the commissary, which was their base camp and had at least one light on. The figure walked to where one investigator had left her laptop computer up and running, and appeared to turn it off. When they reached the commissary and got inside, they found no one at all, but the computer had been turned off. Since it was completely off, and not just in "sleep" mode, someone, or something, had to have turned it off.

DPI's conclusion is that Fort Lincoln is haunted. If you want to visit Fort Lincoln yourself, be sure to tour the Custer House, and consider spending a night at the campground there, so that perhaps you can wander around the buildings after dark, and find your own spooky story!

The Maltese Cross Ranch Cabin, Medora

Just inside the Medora entrance to the South Unit of Theodore Roosevelt National Park, in the Badlands of western North Dakota, sits the Maltese Cross Ranch Cabin, built by Theodore Roosevelt and Sylvaine Ferris, his ranch foreman, not long after he arrived in the town then called Little Missouri (or Little Misery by some inhabitants). It took a long and interesting journey before it arrived there.

Roosevelt's first home in Dakota Territory, in 1883, was actually a log stockade shack – logs placed vertically to the ground, with split shingles for a roof, and he called his land the Chimney Butte Ranch. He soon changed the ranch name to the Maltese Cross, his name for the symbol he used to brand his cattle, and he and Ferris built a better cabin, with horizontal logs, some taken from the Little Missouri River as they were floated down by the Northern Pacific Railroad, with a planked floor for the main floor's three whitewashed rooms (Roosevelt's bedroom, a living room, and a kitchen), and a loft for the cowboys to sleep in. This second cabin was much warmer in the long and bitterly cold Dakota winters. The cabin also had a root cellar and a "factory cut cedar-shingled roof" over the loft.

Roosevelt built another cabin on another ranch during his years in Dakota Territory – the Elkhorn Ranch, about thirty-five miles north of Little Missouri, which by then had been renamed Medora, after the wife of the Marquis de Mores who had made his home and business there. That cabin was a cottonwood log cabin, one of the finest in its day, and it was farther from the main trails than the Maltese Cross. Roosevelt did most of his Dakota writing there. But by the time he became President that cabin had disappeared, and all that remains today at the Elkhorn ranch site are a few foundation blocks.

Theodore Roosevelt was already living in the east full-time by 1886, pursuing a career in politics, but he kept ownership of his ranch business. After losing most of his cattle in the winter of 1886-87, the coldest and snowiest winter on record for North Dakota, he was unable to make up his losses. His final visit to the Elkhorn ranch was in 1892. He sold his interest in the two ranches to his ranch manager, Sylvaine Ferris, in 1898, and gave up his ranching dreams. He later said that if he hadn't spent those years in Dakota, he never would have become President.

The Maltese Cross cabin was Ferris's home for a while, then was sold again, and in 1903, the state of North Dakota bought the cabin to refurbish it and display it at the 1904 World's Fair in St. Louis, Missouri. After the fair was over, the cabin was shipped to Portland, Oregon, for a "Lewis and Clark" anniversary exposition, where it stayed for 137 days.

Finally, in 1906, the Maltese Cross cabin came home to North Dakota. It was exhibited at the Fargo State Fair Grounds for two years. In 1908, the cabin was moved to the State Capitol Grounds in Bismarck, having been seen by an estimated 2 million people in its travels. Many of the bottom logs had rotted or were lost or stolen, and some of the other logs were gone as well. It was unprotected on the grounds, and was neglected and vandalized. The Bismarck chapter of the Daughters of the American Revolution (DAR) saw this as a chance to save what they felt was a North Dakota "shrine" of sorts. In 1919, they asked the State Board of Administration to let them restore and maintain the cabin. They were given permission, with the condition that the work be overseen by the State Historical Society of North Dakota (SHSND).

Their fundraising continued for many years, and in 1923, the Maltese Cross Ranch Cabin was ready to show off again, with money to maintain its condition. They had not merely made it look as it had in its first incarnation (Roosevelt's photos from that time were a great help), but they had also been able to get many of the original furnishings, and where they couldn't, they found period pieces that were similar to those used during Roosevelt's occupation of the cabin.

In 1949, the state legislature passed a bill to move the cabin to the new Theodore Roosevelt National Park located in the Badlands of western North Dakota. The National Park Service (NPS) agreed to maintain the cabin, but the legislature hadn't provided the funds to move it, so it remained in Bismarck until July of 1959, following the 1958 Theodore

Roosevelt Centennial. It was sent by train to Medora, where the NPS restored it again, inside and out.

These days the cabin looks much as it did when Roosevelt lived in it. And apparently it still feels like home to Teddy. Promised anonymity, certain Park employees tell stories of many people who, on their way out of the park right around closing time, tell the ranger at the entry station how much they enjoyed the Roosevelt re-enactor at the Maltese Cross cabin, how much he looked like the photos of Teddy, and how he stayed in character the entire time he talked to them. Which would have been great, if there had actually been a re-enactor there. Others report hearing a bluff and hearty laugh coming from the cabin when it's empty, and seeing lights in the windows after dark, when the park is closed. Other visitors have noted a shadowy figure inside the cabin that vanishes as they enter, or is seen out of the corner of the eye as it moves around the back of the cabin.

Theodore Roosevelt recalled his years in North Dakota as some of the best in his life. He went from being a sickly young man with some insecurities to a strong, healthy, confident man fit to lead his country. Is it any wonder, then, that he stays in his old Badlands home?

Chateau de Mores, Medora

In the spring of 1883, the dashing young Frenchman, Antoine Amedee Marie Vincent Amat Manca de Vallambrosa, the Marquis de Mores, arrived in the town of Little Missouri, ready to build a summer home and a business empire. A former French army officer and noted duelist, De Mores had fallen in love with the beautiful Medora Von Hoffman, daughter of a wealthy New York banker, when her family visited France, and the two married in Cannes, in 1882. Medora wasn't the usual high society miss of her era; she had an adventurous spirit and was known as a bruising rider and big game hunter. They were the perfect couple.

Turning up his nose at the squalor that was Little Missouri, De Mores built his hunting cabin on a bluff on the west side of the river. He would later build a church and a summer home for his in-laws, as well as several small businesses, on the east side of the river and change the name of the town to Medora, after his wife. Medora didn't arrive with him because she was pregnant with their first child, a daughter they named Athenaïs. That August, when the baby was two months old, she came with a train car full of furnishings, some servants, and little Athenaïs to join her husband. She also brought her saddle and her hunting rifle.

The building that the Marquis and his family called their hunting cabin was called the Chateau, or castle, by their neighbors, and the name stuck. It wasn't a true chateau, but a larger version of the typical homes in the region, at least on the outside. The inside was furnished with European luxury. The home had two floors, with a main staircase and a servants' staircase, and twenty-six rooms, including servants' rooms and guest rooms, as well as a private dressing room and study for both the Marquis and Marquise. The living and dining rooms were decorated in the first style of luxury, and the couple, later with their children, had guests for dinner nearly every night. Teddy Roosevelt dined with them a couple of times, and wrote to his sister Alice how much he had enjoyed the fresh fruit served as dessert.

De Mores's business idea was to slaughter cattle from the surrounding ranches at a slaughterhouse in town, then pack the meat into refrigerated train cars and ship meat, rather than cattle on the hoof, to Chicago and points east. He and Medora's father, the Baron Von Hoffman, both invested in the business, although the Marquis put nearly everything he had into it. At that time, obviously, modern refrigeration didn't exist, so the Marquis built a series of ice houses every 100 miles along the train route to Minneapolis and Chicago, to replace the ice that kept the meat from spoiling. He also established a stagecoach route, the Medora to Deadwood stage, betting on the continued gold rush in the Black Hills of South Dakota.

Medora accompanied her husband to the town that bore her name each summer, bringing her daughter, Athenaïs, and son, Louis, born in 1885, along with their nannies. She managed the servants and the running of the home, but she also found time to indulge in her passion for hunting. She shot wolves, mountain lions, coyotes, and even a grizzly bear on a hunting trip to Wyoming. Like those of her husband, her trophies were mounted and displayed in the large hunting room of their home.

By 1886, the Marquis's dreams had died. He had lost somewhere between $500,000 and $1,500,000 in his ranching, slaughterhouse, shipping, and stagecoach ventures. The De Mores family left the Chateau, but they left it with caretakers. De Mores died in 1896, and Medora remained in France. She made one last trip to North Dakota in 1903, with Athenaïs and Louis; her youngest son, Paul, remained in France. She did some hunting, although game was scarcer as the human population and ranched acreage had grown, and held a party to which she invited everyone in Billings County. She then returned to France, where she stayed until her death in 1921.

Caretakers maintained the Chateau until 1936, when the de Mores heirs donated it to the state. It became a State Historic Site, and Paul,

Medora's youngest son, helped with the refurbishing and donated many of the original furnishings, including fine china and crystal glassware, as well as a portrait of Medora painted before her marriage. The Chateau is now one of the major tourist attractions in the town of Medora.

There are those who say that Medora returned to her hunting lodge one more time, after her death, and that the Chateau is where her spirit stays. Many mornings the tour guides find the impression of a body on Medora's side of the bed she had shared with her husband. Her silver brush set is frequently rearranged. One story is that a guide had set the dining room table first thing in the morning, before the Chateau was open for visitors, but apparently Medora wasn't satisfied with the way the silverware was set out, so she rearranged it. People who live in the town say that there are often lights up at the Chateau at night, and that sometimes, on a moonlit night, a woman in white is seen on the porch that surrounds two sides of the house. Others say they've seen a woman in a split leather skirt riding sidesaddle through the Badlands, with a rifle sheathed on her horse – a woman who disappears if you call out to her.

The Chateau de Mores still stands on its hill overlooking Medora.

Many of the employees who work at the Chateau will tell you that they often feel watched, and judged, as they ready the house for the daily tours. But if it is Medora, she isn't an evil spirit. She merely wants her home to be perfect in every detail, just as it was when she lived there.

Medora's studio contains her art supplies and a portrait of her.

Yunker Farm Children's Museum
Fargo

Yunker Farm is a red brick farmhouse built in 1876 by Newton Whitman. Whitman donated his leftover bricks to build a schoolhouse, now on the farm property, that is the oldest rural schoolhouse in the state. In 1905, John A. Yunker, with his second wife, Elizabeth, and his six children, bought the property (480 acres, the farmhouse and its outbuildings) after moving to Fargo from Indiana. Over the next few years, Elizabeth had four children, so the family of twelve – two parents, six sons, and four daughters, inhabited the house.

John Yunker passed away in 1929, and Elizabeth ran the farm and raised turkeys to support her family. A fire broke out at the house in 1945. Although the house was saved, there was a lot of damage to the third floor and the roof, and a lot of remodeling was called for. Elizabeth passed away in 1953, and her son Laurence ran the family farm until 1968. He retired then and sold the farm to the Fargo Airport Authority. In 1974, ownership passed to the Fargo Park district, and the Fargo-Moorhead Junior League turned the former farm into a children's museum.

These days the museum is visited by thousands of children each year. None of them seem to notice anything out of the ordinary. Still, stories persist that the house is haunted. The most common story tells of a presence that watches people working alone in the house, makes the elevator move when no one is in it, and locks or unlocks a door that requires a key, when no one with the key is on the property. This story says that the presence is called Vanessa by museum employees and volunteers, after the mother of the ten children who once lived there.

People who work there now deny any sort of haunting, and it isn't hard to learn that the name of the mother of ten was Elizabeth, not Vanessa. There is no record of anyone dying in the home, although a haunting doesn't always require that someone die in a place, just that they lived there. Given the total lack of any paranormal activity, and the wrong name used in the story, this "haunting" can probably be considered an urban legend.

Yunker Farm House is now a children's museum in Fargo.

Coghlan Castle
East of St. John in Rolette County

There's an old saying that a man's home is his castle. Cornelius "Con" Maurice Coghlan made it a truth for his own home by hiring Canadian stone mason Thomas Bowyer to build him and family (wife Sadie, a daughter, Marjorie, born 1909, and a son born later) a castle, complete with a turret and tower windows. It was built of native fieldstone and is located in northern North Dakota. It took three years, 1906 to 1909, to complete the home. The stone exterior walls are two feet thick, and the inside has beautiful woodwork done by Coghlan's brother John, who had done elaborate woodwork for passenger and Pullman railroad cars of that period.

Coghlan Castle was built of native fieldstone in northern Rolette County.
Photo courtesy of Mariah Masilko.

The Castle sits on a hill east of St. John. It was modern for its time; it had running water, a hot water heater, a bathtub and indoor toilet, and a skylight in the upstairs bathroom. The first floor has five main rooms, including a living room with a diamond pattern wood inlaid floor, done by John Coghlan. In addition to the main rooms, the first floor has a foyer and a butler's pantry off the kitchen. There are five bedrooms on the second floor, including the turret room whose little dormer windows help provide light. A grand polished wood staircase sweeps up to the second floor from the foyer, while a servants' staircase goes up the back of the house from the kitchen.

While the Coghlans lived there, they held plenty of parties, especially after 1919, when prohibition gripped the U.S. The Castle is just a few miles from the Canadian border, and it would have been a quick trip for the Irish Catholic Con Coghlan to drive up and bring back illegal liquor. The Roaring Twenties were a time for jazz music and flappers with waved bobbed hair, the Charleston, small moustaches, and spats.

Coghlan Castle is empty now, although the building has been placed on the National Register of Historic Places, and is being restored by the SHSND. The windows are mostly broken, and what was once the lawn is now a hay field. The wind blows through the house, and autumn leaves skitter through the skylight as days grow shorter in the fall. Still, if you're near the Castle after dark, you may hear the faint echoes of jazz music and clinking glass, laughter and conversation; the scent of cigars may float from the windows, mingled with a hint of women's perfume. Don't stay too long; this is a fey place. If you spend a night, you just might vanish under the hill the Castle sits on, to join the Coghlan family and the other Celtic spirits who don't feel at all out of place beneath the stone walls of Coghlan Castle.

The Ghost Hunter's Haunted House
Grand Forks

It's ironic when a paranormal investigator finds that the house she lives in is haunted, but that's what happened to Lorrie Hanson, a member of Grand Forks ghost hunting group, Night Light Paranormal Investigations (NLPI). At least she knew who to turn to for help!

On September 30, 2009, reporter Joel Porter, of WDAZ TV in Grand Forks accompanied the members of NLPI as they investigated the home of one of their own. Lorrie told the reporter that she believes she is being followed by an entity or spirit. Some of her experiences included having fans turning on and off by themselves, and seeing a shadowy figure going from her office to her bedroom.

The reporter watched as members of NLPI went through the house, setting up cameras, video cameras, and voice recorders. Next, one group went through with an EMF (electromagnetic field) detector, and a thermometer to check for cold spots. A second group, led by NLPI founder Patty Newark, took still photos and voice recordings as they tried to contact whatever may be lurking in Lorrie's home.

Newark explained that sometimes spirits linger because they have unfinished business, or because they died suddenly and unexpectedly and don't understand that they are dead. It's NLPI's mission to help such spirits find closure, or find their way to "the light" where they should be, instead of among the living. Lorrie wants to know why she's being followed, and if there is anything she can do to help the spirit cross over. NLPI has been doing this, without charging those who need their help, since about 2003.

As they went through their sound recordings the next day, they did catch a few EVPs that seem to be a male voice. But the activity at the home hasn't stopped.

Haunted House on the Prairie
Near Bottineau

Bottineau County, on the northern boundary of North Dakota, is home to Carla and James Swenson and their son, Bob; their two daughters have left the nest. The Swenson house is a three-story prairie-style home built around 1905 that the Swensons moved from its original location to their property in the hills of Turtle Mountain north of the town of Bottineau. Listed on the National Register of Historic Places, their home has the air of a comfortable, lived-in home. But Carla feels that it may not be just her family living there, and she talked about it to the *Lake Metigoshe Mirror*.

When they first moved the house, they needed to put a lot of sweat equity into it before they could live in it. Once her children were asleep in their rooms, Carla would often leave the house they were living in at the time and go up to work on the house. One night as she was heading back home, she saw a light in a window upstairs, when she was certain that she'd turned them all off. She looked closer, and saw a figure in the window. That was enough to deter her from going back in to turn it off, and in fact, she decided, after that, she wouldn't work at the house at night. A worker they'd hired told her that he had seen a similar figure in a different window when no one was upstairs.

Both of the Swenson daughters, although now living elsewhere, have had their own experiences in the house. Kayla said that one night she was awakened by a child's voice calling, "Mom, Mom," like it was trying to wake her up. She checked around the room, but no one was there or in the hall. Another time, a friend was visiting her, and went into the bathroom. As the friend reached for the light switch, the light came on by itself. And eerily, a doorknob turned in her hand, when no one was on the other side of the door.

Daughter Allie refuses to stay in the house when she visits; she stays at the family's lake cabin at nearby Lake Metigoshe instead. Her experience included the family's cat. Allie was home alone, watching television while waiting for a friend, when she heard a three note chord played on the family's piano. She looked into the dining room where the piano is kept, and no one was there, though the family cat was sitting on the bottom step of the stairway to the second floor. She went back to her seat on the living room couch only to hear the same chord play a few minutes later, and this time when she opened the door to the dining room, the cat streaked past her out of the room and into the kitchen, where it hid under the table. Allie returned to the living room and heard the chord play one more time. That was it for her; she put on her shoes, left the house, and drove into town.

Carla too has had experiences since moving into the house. Footsteps are heard on all floors, both at night and during the day, and tapping sounds on the windows are common. But the creepiest phenomenon has happened to her two or three times when her husband James wasn't home. She was in bed in their third floor bedroom, when she felt what seemed like someone trying to get into bed beside her. The bed went down, like someone sat down on it. She says she put her head under the covers with the theory that if she could ignore it, it would go away.

Carla Swenson isn't a fan of scary movies or ghost hunting television shows, which, she says, probably helps her deal with the activity in her house. But since nothing has broken and no one has been hurt, she says the "presence" can stay if it behaves itself. The best part for her? When I first spoke with Carla, her husband James hadn't experienced anything. Since then, though, he has seen the swinging doors to the kitchen move by themselves, when there was no breeze and no rush of air from the heater or air conditioner. While James is still a non-believer in ghosts, he now admits that something strange is happening.

The House With Many Questions
Grand Forks Area

A woman who wants her name and address to remain private contacted the Grand Forks group Night Light Paranormal Investigations (NLPI) for assistance in 2009. Her house, which was built around 1917, has not been feeling homelike to her. She sees shadowy figures of animals and people, hears voices and crying in the night, and one morning she awoke with pain in her back. When she looked at it in the mirror, her back was covered with scratches.

The house is old and has had many owners. Joys and sorrows, peace and violence, comedy and tragedy have all visited this house. NLPI went in to investigate, in the hope of debunking what they could, and helping any remaining spirits to move on or cross over into the realm where they belong.

A private home in Grand Forks has many mysteries. *Photo by Lorrie Hanson, courtesy of Night Light Paranormal Investigations.*

They set up video cameras and voice recorders, and two teams armed with still cameras and voice recorders took turns being on the main floor and in the basement. One of the photos they took when they conducted the client interview seemed to show the shadow of a human-like figure. They tried to recreate that shadow but weren't able to do so. During an EVP session, a member of the team asked who the shadow person was. When they subsequently reviewed the tape, they found that there was a response, a childlike female voice saying, "I'm sorry... it was him." On the video camera left in the basement, which also records an audio track, they picked up what sounds like stamping feet right beside the camera during a time when no one was in the basement.

One of the team members, a girl of 19, says she has been talking to ghosts or dead people all her life. She is on one of the video cameras, holding the hand of an unseen child that she says is a little boy. He told her that at one time there were two big people who argued all the time. There were children, he said, and he misses playing with them. The team member felt that the child had died in the house a very long time ago, and NLPI is now researching past owners of the house to see if they can learn his identity.

NLPI feels that the activity is probably not demonic, but that a malevolent spirit is in the house, along with the child and possibly other spirits. They hope that with another investigation and possibly a blessing by a member of the clergy, the house can be cleared and the woman can have some peace. In the meantime, it is truly a house with many unanswered questions.

This photo taken inside the Grand Forks home shows the edge of a human-shaped shadow. *Photo by Lorrie Hanson, courtesy of Night Light Paranormal Investigations.*

A Ghostly Roommate
Bismarck

In the Cathedral Historic District in Bismarck, you'll find houses dating from the late 1800s to around 1935. Most of them show different architectural styles of the period, or have some unique feature; the neighborhood is on the National Register of Historic Places as a district, but each house is considered historic too. Houses range from small bungalows and ranch-style homes to large prairie farm type architecture, and many other styles. On any given block in the neighborhood you may find Craftsman, Mission, Georgian, and Neo-Classical architecture. The district is a very popular place to live for those willing to live with the endless demands of an older home, and most people who live there, live there for life.

A deceased former owner seems to still linger in this Bismarck home.

One of these houses is a small, one-story, craftsman-style bungalow built around 1929. Over the years it had many owners, but the owners who stayed the longest, a period of nearly thirty years, were a childless couple that the current owner wants to call the Andersons. Mr. Anderson died first, and his widow remained in the home for another nine years, tending her roses and keeping her home as neat as a pin. When she passed away in late 1993, the house, along with the rest of her estate, went to a distant nephew, whose attorney put the house on the market. It was purchased in 1994, and between then and when the current owner bought it in 1997, it had three different owners, probably a record for homes in this area.

The current owner, who asked to be called Anne, knew nothing of the house's history when she purchased it and moved in. A Bismarck native, she'd been living out of state for nearly twenty years, and returned to the city intending to stay. After she'd been in the home for about three weeks, she said she woke up quite suddenly. Her next-door neighbor had motion-activated security lights which went off frequently, and unfortunately one of them went straight through her bedroom window, so even in the darkest night, there was often light in her room, and there was light that night.

At the foot of her bed, she saw an elderly woman. Her first thought was that this woman might be slightly senile or have Alzheimer's disease, and had wandered into the wrong home, although she was sure she'd locked all the doors, and she had a large dog who should have barked. She asked the woman if she was lost, and the woman promptly vanished. At that point Anne realized that her visitor hadn't been alive. Anne has had some paranormal experiences in her life, so isn't a complete skeptic when it comes to ghosts, but she wasn't really ready to say her house was haunted at that point. Maybe she'd dreamed it, she thought.

Over the next couple of weeks, she woke up frequently and saw this woman at the foot of her bed. The woman often looked angry, and sometimes shook a finger at Anne, as if she was scolding a naughty child. After the first appearance, when the woman had seemed solid and real, the woman became slightly transparent and looked, well, ghostly.

Having coffee with an elderly neighbor one day, Anne was looking through some of the neighbor's photos of friends and the gardens each of them prized. On one of the photos she saw the woman that she'd been seeing in her bedroom. She asked the neighbor who that woman was, and was told that it was Mrs. Anderson, who had died a few years ago in her bedroom – the very bedroom Anne now slept in. Her home was still referred to by long-term neighbors as the Anderson home, and neighborhood gardeners spoke almost reverently of Mrs. Anderson's roses, none of which still graced the garden.

With her ghostly visitor identified, Anne began to do something that, she says, made her feel rather silly. She would sit on her bed before going to sleep, and speak to Mrs. Anderson. She told the spirit that this house belonged to her now, not to Mrs. Anderson. She told Mrs. Anderson that there was a much better place for her to be, and that she should look around her for a light, and when she saw it, that she should walk into it. She explained to Mrs. Anderson that the light was pure love, and that it wasn't anything to fear, and she asked Mrs. Anderson to leave her alone. After a couple of weeks of this, the spirit stopped appearing.

Things stayed quiet, paranormal-wise, in Anne's home until 2002. After a major rain and hailstorm left her with water in her basement, she hired a plumber to put in a sump pump. This required breaking the cement of the basement floor, something that hadn't been done since the house was built. It wasn't long afterward that new things started happening.

According to Anne, the first manifestations were lights turning on in the basement room directly under her bedroom and in her bedroom closet. This wasn't a wiring problem; the switches were moved up, and had to be moved down to turn the lights off again. At first she thought perhaps she'd left the lights on herself, accidentally, but as it continued she realized that once her bedroom lights were turned off, she'd be able to see the line of light around her bedroom door, or the glow coming through the old heater vent in her bedroom floor. She'd check that before going to sleep, so if the lights were on when she woke up, she'd know that it wasn't her doing. A friend suggested that her large dog might have been pushing the light switches up, but the dog showed no interest in light switches during the day, and refused to go into the basement.

Another thing she noticed was that when she was in the basement to do laundry, she felt as if someone, or something, was behind her, watching her. The location of the watcher seemed to be the sump pump, and she described the watcher as "malevolent." To this day she only does laundry during daylight hours, and is in the basement for the shortest possible time period.

Eventually, new things began to happen. Small items like earrings or watches would disappear, and then reappear somewhere completely different. One night she left her favorite pair of earrings on the night stand before she went to sleep. She searched for them for several days without finding them, until one morning she went into the kitchen to start the coffeepot and found the earrings sitting in the sink. She had used the sink during the period of her search. A book disappeared from her bedroom, and she found it only accidentally, when she went into the second bedroom, a room she uses mainly for storage, to get something from the closet there, and found the book lying centered on the rug.

Anne began hearing whispering voices at night that seemed to be coming from the heater vent. She heard what she thought were both male and female voices, but couldn't make out any words. She started hearing footsteps coming slowly and with determination (her word) up the stairs; at those times, her dog often would often put its ears back and raise its hackles in fear, so she knew, or felt she knew, that she wasn't the only one hearing them. The first couple of times she looked and found no one on the stairs, so she stopped looking.

Events began to accelerate in early spring of 2009. First, she woke up around 3 a.m. one morning, and heard water running in the bathroom next to her bedroom. She went in, and the room was icy cold. It's usually the warmest in the house in winter weather because it's small and has a large radiator, and she keeps the door closed to keep the dog out. The cold water tap was on in the bathtub, and the water level was almost up to the top. The tub had no built-in stopper; if she wanted to take a bath she had to put a rubber mat across the drain. The mat wasn't in the tub; it was in its usual place on the corner of the tub's rim. She reached into the cold water to see if there was something blocking the drain, and although she found nothing, she said, "It was like breaking a spell. Suddenly the water started to drain, the room was warm, and the lights came on."

She knew she hadn't turned the water on, and it hadn't been on when she went to bed, or she would have heard it. She began to get frightened, but didn't know where to go for help.

The last straw came about a week later. She was awakened suddenly but completely by a sound she couldn't identify. A side sleeper, on her right side with her back to the bedside table, she rolled onto her back and started to sit up. As she did that, she felt something she describes as "long and flat" strike her face. She describes falling back onto her pillows, covering her head with her right arm, screaming, and reaching for the bedside light to turn it on. When the light came on, she was alone in the room except for her dog, who was trying in vain to wedge itself into the small space between the night stand and the wall, ears flattened and hackles up. She got up and took her large and heavy flashlight, and walked through the rooms on the main floor, the dog following her. No one was there, the doors were locked and dead-bolted, and all the windows were locked. In the bathroom mirror, she noted red spots on her forehead and cheekbone.

She spent the rest of the night on the couch with her dog, sleeping fitfully. In the morning, the red spots had faded but her eye was blackened. She contacted TAPS, The Atlantic Paranormal Society made famous by their television series, "Ghost Hunters," on the SyFy network. They referred her to a TAPS affiliate in Colorado. Because that organization felt that Anne's case had become urgent, and they weren't able to get to North Dakota quickly, they found a group that they felt had the same goals as they and TAPS did: to "debunk" anything that they could – that is, to prove that it had a normal rather than paranormal cause – and to help deal with anything that they couldn't debunk.

Dakota Paranormal Investigators (DPI) arrived a couple of weeks later (roads were a problem that spring because of major flooding across the state), and set up their equipment to do an investigation. From 9 p.m. until about 2:30 a.m., they investigated with video and still cameras, infrared cameras, digital voice recorders, digital EMF detectors, and K-2/EMF detectors. One of the first findings came on the walk-through tour of the house. In the basement, just above the washer and dryer, is a copper pipe or conduit; it was giving off a digital EMF reading of over 40. [For reference purposes, a "normal" EMF is from nothing to maybe 0.1. High EMF readings can cause headaches, nausea, excessive fatigue, dizziness, hallucinations, and feelings of paranoia.]

For Anne, that finding was a huge relief. She wasn't crazy, and there was a rational explanation why she felt watched each time she did laundry. Since high EMF levels can be health hazards, she has plans to hire an electrician and get something done to reduce the levels leaking from that pipe.

Other than that, and high EMF readings on the living room floor each time the heater kicked on, it was a very quiet night. Just before the end of the investigation, Anne was downstairs with two female DPI investigators. They were holding the K-2 meter and asking that whoever was there, possibly Mrs. Anderson, light up the lights on the K-2. Nothing happened, as nothing had happened for hours, until Anne said, "I know you were a gardener, Mrs. Anderson. Did you have any other hobbies? Did you do hardanger?" (Hardanger is a Norwegian cutwork embroidery craft.) At the word "hardanger" all the lights on the K-2 meter lit up. The investigator holding the K-2 handed it to Anne and urged her to continue asking questions. Anne asked, "Are you angry that I asked you to leave?" and the lights lit up again. The next question was, "I'm sorry I did that. Can you forgive me?" Once more all the lights lit up. Anne was starting to ask another question when one of the male investigators came into the basement room, the one with the sump pump, where they were sitting. She finished her question but nothing happened. As if whatever was answering had been frightened off by the male person in the room, they got no further K-2 responses, so called it a night.

DPI felt that the limited number of K-2 responses gotten at the end of the investigation weren't enough to qualify as paranormal activity, although Anne is convinced that Mrs. Anderson was communicating with her. Anne knows that DPI is just a phone call away, and very little has happened since the investigation. Anne says that occasionally the basement light will turn on by itself (or by Mrs. Anderson!) but if it bothers her she'll loudly reprimand the ghost and the basement light will turn off again. And she has promised to plant some new rose bushes next summer.

Anne feels that if Mrs. Anderson, or whoever the entity is, is willing to stay in the basement, and not to cause her any harm, she can live with an occasional light going on, and occasional whispering voices. She does wonder, though, if a second investigation might turn up some paranormal activity. "It's not like a light switch," she says. "You can't just turn it on and off. Things happen when they happen, and there are more nights when nothing happens than when something does. So I'm not totally convinced that there's nothing here but me." She remains grateful for the support of DPI, and for the knowledge that they'll come again if she needs them.

Everything remained remarkably calm in the house over the summer and following winter, although lights occasionally turned themselves on and off.

Once, she said, she was tired of the basement light, which had turned itself on, then off, several times as she was trying to sleep. Out of patience, she yelled, "Cut it out! I'm trying to sleep!" To her amazement, the light went out, and didn't go back on. She wasn't sure if she should be relieved or scared, but it did stop that activity—for a while.

But the following spring she endured another disturbing incident. While working on her computer late one night, with her dog lying by her side, she heard those heavy footsteps on the stairs again. Her dog suddenly leaped up and dove under the table, curling itself into a ball.

Anne stood up and looked into the kitchen, where the entryway and landing of the stairway was, and then back down at her dog. She says that when she looked at her dog, she saw a swift movement in the kitchen out of the corner of her eye.

In the next instant, her left arm was grabbed by what felt like a cold, callused hand, and her arm felt icy cold, although the rest of her body felt normal. She says she felt around her left arm with her free right hand and felt nothing but cold air.

She yelled, "Let me go!" several times. Then, according to her, a thought "popped into her head," one that she wouldn't have come to on her own. It was to invoke the name of Jesus. She shouted, "In the name of Jesus, I command you to let me go!" and her arm was released, and the temperature returned to normal.

That night her arm showed red marks where the invisible hand had held it, but by morning it was a large bruise, one that even her neighbor said looked like the mark of a hand and fingers. It got darker over the next few days, and everyone who saw it said it looked like a hand print.

Anne wasn't sure what to think; she had read that ghosts don't harm people, and that only demons respond to a command made in the name of God or Jesus. She really didn't want to think that there was anything demonic in her home. From a Catholic neighbor, she got a small bottle of Holy Water, and sprinkled it on herself and around the house, commanding "unclean spirits and demons" to leave her and her home, in the name of the Father, the Son, and the Holy Spirit.

Anne plans to ask her minister again to bless her house, and if that individual should refuse, to turn to her neighbor's priest. She also plans to contact a demonologist for assistance. When asked by a friend if she would move, she said that she feels her house is her home, and that she would first try to rid it of anything dangerous. And how, she asks, could she, in any good conscience, sell a house that might hold a demon?

Anne's struggle continues, although when last contacted, she said that all was quiet.

Richardton's Memorial Hospital is now a long-term care
facility, but ghostly memories still haunt the hallways.

Haunted Hospitals and Clinics

Since hospitals were places of dying almost as often as they were places of healing in the past, as well as areas of psychological trauma and intense feelings, it's probably not surprising that so many of them are haunted. Indeed, what may be more surprising is that there are hospitals that aren't haunted. But small as the state's population may be, North Dakota has its share of haunted hospitals.

St. Alexius Hospital

Bismarck

St. Alexius was not just the first hospital in Bismarck, it was the first hospital to open in Dakota Territory. In 1878, a group of Benedictine nuns arrived from St. Joseph, Minnesota, to start a girls school. Realizing the desperate need for a facility to serve the sick and needy in Bismarck, their Abbot, Alexius Edelbrock, bought what had been the Lanborn Hotel, on the corner of 6th Street and Main Avenue in downtown Bismarck, from local businessmen (and shady politicians) Alexander McKenzie and Robert Mellon. After a $30,000 remodeling job, the four-story brick building opened as a hospital, and started with fifteen beds and a coal stove in each room.

Sister Boniface, born Mary Ann Timmins, arrived in Bismarck in 1892 to take charge of St. Alexius Hospital. In 1915, the hospital had several physicians on staff, and outgrew their existing quarters. They moved to the present location on the corner of 9th Street and Rosser Avenue, and the hospital continues to grow.

Until her death in 1937, Sister Boniface continued to manage the hospital, whose patients and visitors have included Theodore Roosevelt, Sitting Bull's son, President Woodrow Wilson, and after Sister Boniface's day, President John F. Kennedy. The focus of the Benedictine sisters, however, was always on the ordinary people of the region, not the wealthy or famous. Sister Boniface made sure no one was ever turned away.

Despite her heavy management and finance workload, Sister Boniface still found time to visit many of the hospital's patients during late evenings, making sure that they were comfortable and had everything they needed. It appears that although she is no longer living, Sister Boniface still walks the halls of St. Alexius, checking on patients.

The Benedictine sisters still run the hospital, and make up some of the nursing staff. Times have changed, though, and the nuns no longer wear the wimples and full-length habits of Sister Boniface's day. Except, of course, for Sister Boniface. Many patients, especially those near the oldest part of the hospital, report late-night checks by a kind, if quiet, nun in full habit, who seems to glide silently in and out of rooms and through the hallways. Those patients who later see the portrait of Sister Boniface near the main entry immediately recognize her as their midnight visitor.

St. Alexius was the first hospital in Bismarck.

Does Sister Boniface linger, still watching over the hospital she ran for so many years, and making sure that patient care continues to meet her high standards? Or are patients, perhaps under the influence of pain or sleep medications, seeing what they expect to see in a Roman Catholic hospital? Spend a night at St. Alexius and see for yourself.

St. Joseph's Hospital
Dickinson

St. Joseph's hospital in Dickinson, a major city in the southwest part of North Dakota, is a twenty-five-bed Critical Access Hospital with a Level Four Trauma Center. The hospital was founded by the Sisters of the Holy Cross in 1912. Dickinson had been growing steadily since its founding in 1880 as a stop on the Northern Pacific Railroad. Until St. Joseph's was built, the nearest hospital was in Bismarck, nearly 100 miles away. The Mother House of the Sisters of the Holy Cross was in Switzerland, and most of the nuns who came to serve at St. Joseph's Hospital were Swiss.

The hospital ran smoothly, getting Dickinson through the Spanish influenza outbreak of 1918-19, and those admitted to the hospital were what you'd expect in a mainly rural area. Farm injuries, childbirth, and illnesses like heart disease and pneumonia took up most of the time of the Sisters. They worked as nurses, cooks, laundresses – any job that needed to be done, the dedicated nuns would do.

In February of 1926, a sudden illness struck at the heart of the hospital – the nuns. Six of them became ill with a fever, chest congestion, and difficulty breathing. Although the doctors tried everything they knew how to do, nothing stopped the illness. On February 15, two of the nuns, Sisters Ambrosina Haegele and Anaclete Huwiler died. The next day, Sister Fedele Donati joined them in death. On February 19, Sister Deocara Sicwart succumbed, and three days later, on February 22, Sister Secunda Hackl was the last to die. The sixth nun, Sister Hildebrandis Flury, had not been as sick as the others, and she didn't die. She lived for another eight years.

The doctors and laboratory technicians analyzed everything the Sisters had come in contact with, but nothing was found to be giving off anything poisonous. Finally an autopsy was performed on one of the deceased nuns. The doctor who performed the autopsy found that her brain was inflamed, her kidneys had failed, and there were lesions in her brain as well as one in a kidney. The acting dean of the University of North Dakota's School of Medicine, Dr. H.M.Banks, looked at the findings and concluded that the nuns had died from some infectious type of encephalitis. The coroner's jury, when given all the information from the illnesses and the post-mortem examination, including a discussion of the only similar case then on record, concluded that the Sisters had died of the rare *Encephalitis lethargica*. All five of the nuns were buried side by side in St. Patrick's Cemetery in Dickinson.

But what about the sixth nun, Sister Hildebrandis? According to the *Dickinson Press*, she had not been well since 1926, when her five sisters had died. On February 10, 1934, she died of pneumonia. Some of the nurses and physicians felt that her immune system had been impaired by her battle with encephalitis in 1926; others felt that she was distressed over the deaths of her five sisters eight years before.

Patients in the years following 1934 noticed a ghostly figure in a nun's habit visiting patient rooms – but only the rooms in which the five dead sisters had breathed their last. Staff at the hospital believe that Sister Hildebrandis may also haunt the morgue, looking for the bodies of her sisters. It seems the elevator is often called to the morgue and opens when no one is working there, and the elevator door can only be called to and opened from inside the morgue, with a key. The security tape shows the doors opening, according to a member of the security staff who asked to remain anonymous. Frequently the tape shows only snow in the minutes before the elevator arrives in its nocturnal visits. In unused patient rooms, call buttons that weren't in existence at the time the six nuns lived and died there will signal at night, calling for nurses who no longer come, and voices moan in the darkness. The final part of Sister Hildebrandis's story occurs in St. Patrick's cemetery, where she lies next to the sisters who preceded her in death.

Apparently unrelated hauntings happen in other parts of St. Joseph's hospital. In the oldest area, running footsteps and the sounds of children talking and laughing are heard coming from the basement. The cafeteria rings with the sounds of silverware, dishes, and voices long after it is closed. Whatever haunts the hospital seems to have no intention of leaving.

St. Joseph's Hospital, Dickinson.

The Badlands
Ear, Nose and Throat Clinic
Dickinson

This clinic, which serves the ENT needs of Dickinson and the surrounding area, is said to be haunted. The haunting, if it exists, is poltergeist-like; toilets are flushed when no one is in the restrooms, small pieces of equipment like flashlights disappear and reappear somewhere else; phones ring and when someone answers them, they hear only dead air; supplies like tongue depressors and cottonballs are found spilled from their jars and spread out along the desks in examination rooms, and similar activities are alleged to occur. The actor behind these pranks is a doctor who "disappeared" during a fishing trip, and is believed to be drowned.

All of this would be much less like an urban legend if anyone could name the missing doctor. The clinic is newer than the hospital, and someone there should be able to provide a name. The stories are told most often by teens at the nearby Prairie Hills Mall. Employees of the clinic itself tend to smile and shrug when the haunting is brought up. Is the clinic haunted? I didn't hear anything – but maybe you will.

The Old St. Anne's Guest Home
Grand Forks

Near the Red River in Grand Forks, at 813 Lewis Boulevard, is an imposing four-story structure of brick, topped by a cross and a bell tower. Built in 1907, it served as St. Michael's Hospital until 1952. That year, the Franciscan Sisters of Dillingen bought the building and converted it to a home for the aged, serving over 100 residents. The sisters abandoned it in 1981 when they couldn't meet the state and federal safety codes. They purchased a building on 17th Street, and now serve many more residents than they could at the old building.

Their old building was purchased by a private developer, and was vacant for several years. Eventually, it was renovated and purchased by the Grand Forks Housing Authority, and is in use as low-income apartments. Many of the residents have stories of hauntings.

One of the most popular stories is that the building is haunted by the ghost of a nun named Sister Mary Murphy. It is said that in 1978, shortly before the Sisters moved to the new location, Sister Mary Murphy became seriously depressed. Thinking that she had lost her vocation and been abandoned by God, she flung herself out of the bell tower that tops the old building.

Sister Mary Murphy makes a good story; unfortunately she's an urban legend. No Sister Mary Murphy ever served at St. Anne's Guest Home, and no one ever threw themselves, or fell, from the bell tower at the building on Lewis Boulevard. It is, however, a place that is filled with paranormal activities, which mainly fall into two categories.

St. Anne's Guest House, formerly St. Michael's Hospital, is now low-income housing in Grand Forks. *Photo by Lorrie Hanson, courtesy of Night Light Paranormal Investigations.*

Poltergeist activity is the phenomenon most commonly experienced by those living in the old St. Michael's Hospital/St. Anne's Guest Home building. Small items disappear, only to reappear later in unusual places. Knocking sounds are heard, and doors open and close on their own. One of the members of Grand Forks's Night Light Paranormal Investigations used to live in the building, and he says that while he was there, he learned through some EVPs that a young boy's spirit shared his living space. He reported that this boy was very mischievous, and would hide his glasses and other small things, and knock things over or slide them around.

The other phenomena that occur in the building seem more like a residual haunting (like a film clip; activities repeat themselves but there isn't an intelligent spirit present) than an active one (with the presence of an intelligent entity). Fleeting glimpses of figures in white jackets as well as shadow people have been seen in the upstairs hallways, footsteps are often heard after midnight, and one EVP captured by another member of Night Light Paranormal Investigations sounded like an intercom calling, "Doctor Mulligan! Doctor Mulligan!" Attempts by the investigators to make contact didn't succeed, furthering the theory of a residual haunting. The historical research conducted by the Night Light team uncovered the fact that one of the doctors who helped found St. Michael's Hospital was named Mulligan. Other assorted EVPs were collected during their investigations, but the "Doctor Mulligan" was the clearest, and an obvious link to the building's past.

Between the personal experiences of residents of the former hospital and nursing home and the evidence collected during the investigation by Night Light Paranormal Investigations, there is little doubt that the Old St. Anne's Guest Home/St. Michael's Hospital is haunted. At the least, it is a hot spot of paranormal activity. Visit it at night, if you dare!

Altru Hospital
Grand Forks

Altru Health Systems is the result of the unification of St. Michael's Hospital with Deaconess Hospital in 1971, out of which came a new Medical Park—ninety acres of hospital and clinics, including United Hospital. Planners from United Hospital, the Grand Forks Clinic and the University of North Dakota Medical School decided to join forces to bring better medical care and better medical education to the region. The major flood of 1997 forced the new construction of a cancer center, physical therapy center, and new clinics.

United Hospital was the anchoring facility on the Medical Center, and it was renamed Altru Hospital. Stories of hauntings began almost as soon as the building went into use as United Hospital. One haunting account says that the staff elevator goes up and down during the night shift whether someone is using it or not. If the door happens to open when a staff member is near, a quick look can catch a shadowy figure inside the elevator. In the psychiatric ward, a locked ward, the door alarm goes off frequently through the night, apparently set off by shadow people who then slide out under the door, only to reappear on the other side.

Altru Hospital, Grand Forks. *Photo by Lorrie Hanson, courtesy of Night Light Paranormal Investigations.*

Perhaps most frightening is the physical therapy pool. During the daytime, patients complain about being touched under the water, although they can see nothing there. Wet footprints come out of the pool and walk into the women's locker room, although there are no visible feet making them. At night, the security video has recorded splashing in the pool, although I was informed by an anonymous source that those tapes are deleted when the splashing is noted. Wet footprints also leave the pool at night, sometimes walking around the pool before entering a locker room. In the mornings, wet towels are sometimes found in locker rooms, when the night before all used towels were sent to the laundry facility. There are no reported deaths during either the construction of the pool or the period it's been in use, so no spirit should be present in that area, but the gentle touches, the footprints, and the towels are clear evidence that something paranormal is occurring.

The North Dakota State Hospital

Jamestown

The North Dakota State Hospital is one of two state facilities that were built before North Dakota became a state. The Dakota Territorial Legislature voted to authorize a "hospital for the insane" in 1883, and the facility, located on the south side of a hill overlooking the James River, accepted its first two patients in 1885. Another fifty-eight patients were relocated from Yankton, home of the Dakota Hospital. The superintendent, Dr. O. Wellington Archibald, had previously served as a surgeon at Fort Abraham Lincoln, across the Missouri from Bismarck, the territorial capital. By the end of 1886, the average daily number of patients was 106.

As early as 1886, the hospital administrators began approaching the legislature with a request for more funding; neither the building nor the staff were sufficient to care for so many patients. Despite the hospital's needs, visitors from eastern states described the hospital for the insane as "happy" and "home-appearing." One can only conclude that nineteenth century asylums in the east were truly horrific.

By 1892, residents of that "homey" hospital outside Jamestown were using the attic for additional housing, and forced to sleep two to a bed. Doors were now being locked, and restraints were used as necessary. Although Dr. Archibald threatened that the hospital would close and its patients would be returned to their home counties for care, the legislature did nothing. In 1894, the doctor quit and left in disgust.

The number of patients per day had risen to 401 by 1902, and still the hospital had only one building. The legislature authorized the construction of two new buildings, and construction began, but stopped when the legislature's process of providing the funding was determined to be unconstitutional. Construction finally started again when the legislature taxed each county for the care of its patients, and by 1904 there were two additional buildings, but there was still crowding.

In 1914, the State Hospital adopted a practice common to insane asylums at that time, and began to sterilize their patients. These mentally ill people were called "degenerates" with "moral deficiencies" and doctors at the time believed that their condition would be transmitted to any children they might have. As time passed and the state's population grew, more and more inmates were committed to the hospital, until by 1929, the hospital was treating an average of nearly 1,500 patients a day. Lengths of stay were much longer than they would be today, and treatments were barbaric and ineffective.

The 1930s were turbulent years for North Dakota's economy and politics. Governor William Langer, known to his cronies as "Wild Bill," was elected in 1930, then removed from office when he was arrested on criminal conspiracy and fraud charges, only to be re-elected in 1937 after he was acquitted. The State Board of Administration, which had already created scandal and controversy by the sudden firing of the President of the North Dakota Agricultural College (later North Dakota State University), began to cause problems at the State Hospital, too. In 1939, Fargo's leading newspaper, the *Fargo Forum*, sent a special examiner, Clyde Duffy, to the State Hospital to find out what was actually going on within its dark brick walls and high fences.

What he found was that Langer's followers in the Non-Partisan League (NPL) had fired most of the staff that had been there the longest, and replaced them with people who were owed favors, in the form of jobs, by the party and the governor. This led to a break-down in the running of the hospital, as well as a breakdown of the quality of care provided to the patients. Some patients wept to lose caregivers who had been their as long as they had; others ran away. In part because of Duffy's report, printed in full by the *Fargo Forum*, and in part due to the change in politics at the end of Langer's term of office, the current superintendent of the Hospital, one Dr. F.O. Lorenzen (who had been appointed by Langer), left the hospital.

However, the absence of Lorenzen was no relief to the inmates, whose number swelled to over 4,000 during the 1940s. Strait jackets and other restraints were in common use; "difficult" patients were kept in metal cages or boxes; patients were locked alone in windowless rooms. Those patients able to work were forced to work at least sixty hours a week, many wearing leg-shackles if their work took them out of doors. Conditions in the overcrowded hospital were unsanitary, and the tuberculosis patients were kept with the rest of the population, creating an epidemic similar to the smallpox epidemic that had almost shut the facility down in 1914. Depressed patients were stripped of clothing, sheets, and blankets, anything they might use to take their own lives, and locked in a back ward. Malnutrition was rampant. Cold ice-water baths and electroshock were commonly used to treat schizophrenic patients, depressed patients, and bipolar patients; the last group were often considered to be schizophrenic because of their great mood swings. A mad bedlam ruled many wards due to lack of care and supervision.

The hospital finally began to improve in the 1950s. The state legislature appropriated more money for facilities and staff, and Dr. R.O. Saxvik, who had been working for the State Health Department and who was a greatly respected physician, was placed in charge of the hospital. The failures cited above were turned around with funds and a responsible supervisor, and tranquilizers began to replace electroshock and ice baths. An after-care program was started, making it possible for patients to return home and still receive care, dropping the daily patient census to under 2,000. The two oldest buildings were torn down, and new facilities replaced them.

By 1997, the daily census was down to less than 300 a day. Most of the buildings were no longer in use, and wards were closed in those buildings that were used. At that point, the legislature decided to hand three of the buildings over to the Department of Corrections, and after renovation, they became the James River Correctional Facility, relieving the overcrowding at the State Penitentiary in Bismarck. Now the State Hospital and the Correctional Facility stand together within the fences, and stories about the old buildings began to leak out.

Actually, stories were leaking out in the 1960s, when every North Dakota nursing student was required to spend six weeks doing a psychiatric rotation at the State Hospital. Nearly every student had stories when they came out. So, too, do prisoners released from the James River Correctional Facilities.

What are these stories? As you can imagine, the students and prisoners experience much of what the staff in the 1930s and 1940s did. Maniacal laughter fills one locked ward, night after night. In one of the back wards where the deeply depressed had lain naked on stripped mattresses, to starve and die, there are the sounds of women weeping, sobbing, as their spirits remain locked in the same place that their bodies died. In one small building, children's spirits are heard. Sometimes they laugh and sing nursery rhymes; "Ring Around the Rosie" takes on a new significance after the smallpox epidemic. At other times they shout angrily, or cry in fear or sadness, and call for their mothers, unable to understand why they remain in this grim and dirty brick building. One spirit took particular delight, it seemed, in repeating his suicide during the 1960s; when a new group of nurses arrived, he made sure to appear to all of them, but in different times and places throughout the hospital. He'd drop down suddenly in front of each, dangling from a transparent rope, with bulging eyes and blackened tongue, only to disappear as suddenly as he appeared.

Although nursing students are no longer required to do a rotation in the State Hospital, the prisoners who occupy the renovated former hospital buildings are still there. They too hear crying and weeping. In one building, a grim nurse walks down a hallway; you hear her footsteps, like marching boots, before she appears in her white dress and hat, carrying a basin, and walks past the cells and marches onward. Who she is and where she's going remains her secret.

Another phantom is of yet another suicidal patient. He leaped from the top of one of the buildings that is now a Correctional Facility building, and those prisoners on his side of the building can see his filmy body plummet past their window, his mouth open in a silent scream; he is never seen to hit the ground. According to some of the long-term employees, this man only attempted suicide; when he hit the ground he was alive, but completely paralyzed. He lingered for six months before dying in the State Hospital. He's buried, with others, in an unmarked graveyard on the hospital grounds.

Unless you're a criminal or mentally ill, it's hard to get into the State Hospital to confirm that any of these things ever happened, much less still do. You'll need to find an employee, a nurse, or a former nursing student willing to talk, although you'll have to guarantee anonymity, and hear the stories for yourself.

North Dakota Developmental Center
Grafton

Originally designated the Institution for the Feeble Minded, the North Dakota Developmental Center was opened in Grafton in 1904 to care for and educate people then called mentally retarded. The first twelve patients came from the North Dakota State Hospital. In the 1930s the name was changed to the Grafton State School to put an emphasis on its role as a teaching facility. As its population increased steadily, reaching around 1,600 in the 1960s, some of the patients or clients were sent to the San Haven Sanatorium, a tuberculosis treatment center whose patient population had decreased steadily since a cure for tuberculosis was found. However, like most such facilities, both the Grafton and San Haven centers were overpopulated and underfunded, and following a landmark court decision for the rights of developmentally disabled people, the San Haven Sanitorium was closed completely in 1989, while the Grafton State School underwent extensive remodeling. At about the same time in the 1960s, regular school districts began to provide special education, and later programs to mainstream many of the developmentally disabled, and many of those who would have been at the Grafton State School are now able to study, work, and live in their home communities. The population at any given day in the North Dakota Development Center is now around 150, and the Center is now accredited by the Council on Quality Services for People With Disabilities.

While not as haunted as the State Hospital in Jamestown, the Center does seem to be the focus of some paranormal activity. Staff and residents at the Center sometimes hear crying at night, and a little girl calls for her mother, saying, "Mama! Mama! Come and get me!" in a room used as an arts and crafts room during the day. There are light footsteps in hallways and corridors, and frequently the sound of giggling. In one hallway, a former employee said there was the spirit of a little boy dressed in short pants, who, if you rolled a ball to him, would roll it back. Sometimes objects are moved around in classrooms and teacher's rooms, and small items tend to disappear and reappear elsewhere.

The atmosphere at the Developmental Center, despite the overcrowded and generally poor conditions for patients from its opening through the early 1960s, is considered much lighter than that of the State Hospital. The spirits are believed to be of some of the more childlike patients who apparently became confused after their death, and returned as children to the place they'd spent most of their childhood. Aside from the crying and the call for "Mama," the phenomena are generally light-hearted and playful, and nothing malevolent or frightening exists here.

San Haven Sanatorium
Rolette County

Of all the hospitals in North Dakota, the San Haven Sanatorium for tuberculosis patients is the most eerie. Abandoned now, it once served patients dying from what was, in the past, an incurable illness. Now the winds blow through the windowless abandoned buildings, and the once-beautiful flower beds are home to only weeds. No cattle or chickens remain in the ruins of the barn and the chicken coop. Only memories, and perhaps a few lost souls, live on at San Haven.

Back in 1902, the North Dakota State Board of Health reported that "the state is remarkably free from TB." By 1904, the disease was rampant throughout North Dakota, and by 1908, one of every ten non-violent death was from TB. As it spread through the population, the State Board of Health, along with the legislature, slowly realized that something had to be done. Two physicians, Dr. James Grassick, who became the State Superintendent for Public Health in 1906, and Dr. Fannie Dunn-Quain, who was the first female doctor in the state and whose husband, Dr. Eric Quain, was one of the two founders of Quain and Ramstad Clinic in Bismarck, became advocates for the construction of a sanatorium for TB victims, and traveled throughout the state, diagnosing and educating people about tuberculosis.

Spooky San Haven Sanitorium, abandoned infirmary.
Photo courtesy of Mariah Masilko.

In January of 1909, the legislature acknowledged their hard work, and passed a bill that provided for purchasing land, constructing buildings, and hiring staff for a tuberculosis sanatorium in the state. A site was chosen in northern North Dakota, about two miles north of Dunseith in Rolette County, about fifteen miles south of the Canadian border. The site, on the side of a ridge on the edge of the Turtle Mountains, had relatively high altitude and low humidity, both conditions believed to be beneficial for TB patients. It was protected by hills and trees to the west and north, and offered fresh drinking water from springs and lakes. It also had fertile soil, allowing the sanatorium to grow fruits and vegetables. One hundred additional acres were donated to the state.

In 1911, the legislature appropriated the funds for the bill passed in 1909, and proceeded to build an administration building, cottages, and a barn. Funds were also used to buy dairy cattle and chickens, and for the equipment needed by the sanatorium. In November of 1912, San Haven Tuberculosis Sanatorium opened for its first patients. Over the years, it grew into a small village, with perhaps 600 staff members at any given time, and around 300 patients on average, with admissions, discharges, and deaths on-going.

The San, as it was known to patients and locals, was open to anyone with tuberculosis. If an individual couldn't afford to pay for care and housing, his or her home county would be billed. New patients were isolated for the first forty-eight hours to "rest" while the doctors did two twenty-four-hour sputum tests to confirm the diagnosis of TB. Once it was made, the patient would be assigned to a ward and a program of treatment, which included complete bed rest, fresh air, and a healthy diet. These remained the basic treatment throughout the period that San Haven served as a TB sanatorium. The "fresh air" part of the treatment meant that windows were always open in patient rooms, even during North Dakota winters when temperatures could be as cold as 30 or 40 degrees below zero. Patients also spent time lying outside during the day receiving what their physicians called "heliotherapy," or sun therapy, which the physicians felt would strengthen the patients' immune systems so they could destroy the TB bacilli.

These weren't the only treatments at the San. Others included tuberculin treatments, in which TB bacilli were injected into the patient; the theory behind this was that the injected bacilli would act as a vaccine. Pneumothorax treatments, where a needle injected air into the chest to cause a lung to collapse so it could "rest," were common, and usually performed multiple times. If they weren't as successful as the doctors had hoped, the surgeon would remove several of the patient's ribs, to create the collapsed lung. Lungs could reinflate from the needle treatments, but most patients whose ribs were removed died, slowly and painfully.

Since patients came from all over the state, not all of them received visitors, and only adults could visit. Author Dean Hulse, in his book *Westhope*, described visiting his grandfather when he was a boy. His father would go up to his grandfather's room, and he and his mother would remain outside. He would run to the window nearest his grandfather's second floor room, and shout out to him. Hulse's grandfather was one of the fortunate ones who was mobile enough to reach the window; other patients could barely hear the calls of their children and grandchildren. Hulse's grandfather also was fortunate in that his illness began after the development of an antibiotic treatment for tuberculosis, and after just two months he was released to go home, a healthy man.

In the years between 1912 and 1960, over 1,000 patients died at San Haven. The actual number is much higher; the superintendent was required to make a biennial report to the governor, which included the number of patients who died and those who were released, but several of the reports are missing from the North Dakota State Library. The sad little graveyard on the south part of the property stands as mute testimony to the dead. Many of those released were sent home only to die; knowing that they couldn't help them any further, the doctors at the San would allow them to return to their families, who were given strict instructions on how to avoid being infected themselves.

After the use of antibiotics began in 1949, deaths at San Haven gradually dropped from eighty to ninety per year to only sixteen in 1958, and only five in 1972, the last year that the San was used as a tuberculosis sanatorium. The drop was gradual because many of the patients were already so sick that the antibiotics couldn't help them, and others had immune systems resistant to the antibiotics.

As the number of tuberculin patients dropped through the 1950s and 1960s, the number of patients or "inmates" at the Grafton State School had been rising dramatically. In 1958, "overflow" from Grafton began to be sent to San Haven. In the first decade or so, the Grafton patients were seen as a problem by the nursing staff. With no other way to control them while they treated the TB patients still under their care, the developmentally disabled were often restrained in their beds, allowed out of bed only when their sheets were changed and their bodies examined for bedsores. "Treatment" for these "patients" was non-existent; essentially the San was just a warehouse for bodies. Their care was beyond inhumane; it was appalling.

As advocates fought for better treatment of the developmentally disabled, care gradually improved, and real education took place. Patients with greater abilities began to work in the garden and the barn, while others were taught crafts and basic living skills. In 1973, after the last TB patient left San Haven, management of the facility was turned over to the Grafton State School. Between legislation for better care and the focus on returning the developmentally disabled to their homes with special education classes in mainstream schools, the facility was closed permanently in 1987. In 1992, the Turtle Mountain Band of Chippewa purchased San Haven and the property it stood on with the intent of turning it into a museum or an education facility, but nothing has been done yet, and the crumbling hulks of the main hospital and the other buildings stand empty and alone.

Many people in the area, especially those from nearby Dunseith and from Belcourt on the Turtle Mountain Reservation, believe that San Haven is haunted. There are claims of crying babies, and sightings of "water head babies" (some of the Grafton School patients with hydrocephaly). These small children were severely disabled; most were abandoned at Grafton not long after their birth, and most, back then, died before their second birthdays, joining the tubercular patients in San Haven's graveyard. Others claim to see faces in the now glass-less windows at night, and lights that move from window to window, as if a nurse or orderly were making rounds. Weeping, moaning, and coughing are common sounds still heard coming from the building during the night. The twisted orchard trees, weed-filled flower beds, and dirt-filled former fish pond, along with the collapsed buildings, all appear ghostly in moonlight, even covered with a pure white layer of snow.

San Haven has become a mecca for area teens looking to frighten themselves with ghost hunting. Sadly, the deterioration of the building, with broken floorboards, collapsing ceilings, and empty elevator shafts, has led to at least one tragedy. On October 13, 2001, two young men, exploring the ruins with a group of teens, fell into an elevator shaft. A 17-year-old was killed, and a 16-year-old was severely injured. The Turtle Mountain Band increased security at San Haven, and the Rolette County sheriff stepped up patrols, but it hasn't stopped the ghost hunters. The story of the boy's death has grown and mutated until it has become this: Two boys were chased through the San Haven hospital by an escaped lunatic from Jamestown; he caught one of them, slit his throat, and dumped him into the elevator shaft. The other boy lived only because he ducked his head when the maniac struck, but he still carries the knife scar on his chin. And that is how ghost stories grow.

Whether there are actual ghosts there or only bad memories, San Haven is surely haunted. The foreboding feeling of the place is enough to deter sensitive people even on sunny afternoons. If you want to visit San Haven today, **remember that it is private property and trespassing is not allowed**, and show some respect for the owners and for any lost souls who remain at San Haven.

A lonely prairie cemetery.

Haunted Churches and Spooky Cemeteries

Churches are sacred spaces, and maybe they shouldn't be haunted. But significant events can happen in churches, or their neighboring parsonages, just as they can anywhere else, and troubled, or sometimes helpful, spirits can be left behind. Several churches in North Dakota are said to be haunted, and this chapter looks at three of them.

Who hasn't wanted to visit a cemetery at night, just to scare himself and his buddies? Who hasn't hurried past a graveyard late in the day, when it's getting close to sunset? But why are cemeteries so frightening? They should be the quiet resting place of the dead, or at least their remains. Yet sometimes, very frightening things can happen in what should be peaceful places.

St. George's Episcopal Church
Bismarck

One of Bismarck's oldest churches, St. George's Episcopal Church began as the Protestant Episcopal Church of the Bread of Life in 1873. The first service was held on March 8, 1873, at the Capitol Hotel, where Reverend Charles Swift baptized tiny James Humbert, the son of Lt. and Mrs. Humbert from Camp Hancock. Soon after, Episcopal Bishop Clarkson from Nebraska visited Bismarck, and in 1877, he appointed Rev. J. A. Graham of Brainerd, Minnesota, to hold services on the third Sunday of each month. Those services were held in the old City Hall on 4th Street.

In 1881, a church building was constructed on the corner of Mandan Street and Avenue A. Not long after, in 1887, the church's name was changed to St. George's Episcopal Church, because members felt the original name sounded too "high church." Around 1900, the building was moved to the corner of 3rd and Thayer. A new church was built for the congregation in the 1940s, called St. George's Memorial Episcopal Church, and the original historic building was moved to the Camp Hancock Historic Site on the corner of Main and 1st Streets in the 1960s. It's now open to the public and is sometimes used for weddings or special occasions.

But the story of St. George's doesn't end with its move to the Camp Hancock location. The historic site, which also houses one of the first Northern Pacific Train locomotives and an original Camp Hancock building that was used by the U.S. Weather Bureau, is visited frequently in the summer, and people have been known to mention the dark-robed clergyman who welcomes them to St. George's, or is sometimes seen in the yard beside the church building.

The thing is, there is no clergyman acting as a guide or docent for the old church. Can this man in black be the spirit of one of the early ministers of the church, like Rev. Swift, who started the Episcopalian Church in Bismarck, or perhaps Rev. Miller, the first to have a "mission" in Bismarck? No one knows, because the spectral clergyman never introduces himself. But if you're in Bismarck, stop at Camp Hancock and visit the church yourself. You never know who you might run into.

Historic St. George's Episcopal Church at Camp Hancock, Bismarck.

The Sims Lutheran Church
Sims, Morton County

North of Almont in southern Morton County, about fifteen miles south of Interstate 94 just west of New Salem, there used to be a town called Sims. Even at its peak, the population was small, at just over 1,000. Sims began as a coal mining town, but the vein played out much sooner than expected, and by 1890, only 400 citizens remained. Gradually more people moved away, until the only buildings remaining were the church and the parsonage, which sits beside the church.

The church is still in use on alternate Sundays; when it's not used, the congregation meets in Almont's Lutheran Church. The church is a beautifully maintained white Scandinavian-style prairie church, with a high white steeple. The parsonage was actually built before the church, and services were held in the attic until the church building was completed. Troughs for the parsonage's livestock were carried up each Sunday morning, and turned upside down to use as pews—or kneelers, depending on the sermon.

The parsonage has been unoccupied since 1984, and without residents, it fell into disrepair. But the congregation decided that they simply would not let it become a ruin. With the help of Preservation North Dakota and a grant from Save America's Treasures, the congregation of the Sims church put in the sweat equity to restore the parsonage to its original condition. And when they did, the most famous resident of the Sims church seems to have returned.

The story of the Gray Lady of Sims, as this ghostly resident is known, is one of the most often-told ghost stories in the state. Like a few other stories, it has been written up in books and newspaper articles, and passed from person to person. In the process, a few facts have been left out, and a few others have been incorrectly told. But Bismarck resident Jeani Borchert, the great-niece of Sims's Reverend Lars Dordal, knows all of the story, even the parts that the Dordal family left out when the story began to circulate, and she reveals it here.

In 1916, Reverend Lars D. Dordal and his young wife Bertha Vieland Dordal, along with their three children, Raymond, Harold, and Adeline, moved to Sims from Minnesota. In 1917, Bertha fell ill, and on May 17th, less than two weeks before her 27th birthday, she died. She's buried in the Sims cemetery, with a flat stone that reads only "Mrs. L. Dordal" with the date of her death.

Lars did the best he could, but he was devastated at the loss of his wife, and had no idea how to minister to his flock and raise three small children at the same time. He took some leave from his parish and went to Ada, Minnesota, to visit his brother, Jacob, also a Lutheran minister. As it happened, Jacob's wife was also sick, and they'd hired a girl from town named Clara to help with the housework and care for the Dordal children. Although they never intended it to happen, and Lars still sincerely grieved for his first wife, Lars and Clara fell in love at first sight. The entire Dordal family adored Clara; she was kind, sweet, and loving to everyone. Lars's children clung to her in the absence of their mother.

Lars and Clara married in Minnesota, and then headed back to his church in Sims. Not quite knowing how to explain his quick marriage to his congregation, he decided that they might accept it better if they believed that Clara was Bertha's sister, so that is what he told them.

The Parsonage at Sims, where the Gray Lady walks.

Clara, Lars, and the children were comfortable in the parsonage, but the congregation was no longer comfortable with them, or at least that was the impression that Lars Dordal had. In 1918, he accepted the call of the Lutheran church in Rhame, a small town in extreme southwestern North Dakota, and he packed up Clara and the children, and moved. Later, after two or three other pastors had served in Sims, the Dordals returned to the parsonage. They filled in for a year while the congregation searched for a new minister, then they moved to Hettinger, in southwest North Dakota, and then to Larimore, North Dakota, where Lars worked for the railroad, then preached to four congregations in that town. He and Clara added two children to the family, sons Lyle and Earl.

After the Dordals left for Rhame, the Gray Lady, believed to be Bertha Dordal, began to make appearances. (It should be mentioned that during the Dordal family's second stay in Sims, no sightings of the Gray Lady were reported.) Reverend H.D. Halvorson, who served at Sims after the Dordals left, was a part of the first sighting. He and his wife had a female guest, and they put her in the upstairs room of the parsonage, the same attic, up a winding stair, that had once been used for services. The guest woke in the night, feeling cold, and a woman walked into the room with a blanket, which she spread over the guest. Then the woman left as quietly as she had arrived. The next morning, the guest thanked Mrs. Halvorson for bringing her the blanket. Mrs. Halvorson was startled; not only had she not given the guest a blanket, but she and the guest were the only two living women in the house!

Pastor Gunter Nelson and his wife, Olga, lived in the parsonage in the mid-1930s. Olga saw a gray shape in the upper story of the house, and said that sometimes the outdoor water pump's handle would begin to move up and down by itself – often just as she intended to fetch water or send one of her children for it. Breezes would blow through the downstairs living area even when windows were closed. Later stories reported cupboards opening and closing on their own, and doors and windows that wouldn't stay closed. Under close questioning, it seems that each cupboard tended to open most often when someone needed something from it, and doors opened just before a resident could open it for himself.

While some pastors' wives, like the wife of Reverend Halvorson, were frightened by the appearance of the Gray Lady and insisted that their husbands seek a new parish, Mrs. Nelson felt the present of the spirit as a nurturing one. She believed it was the spirit of Bertha Dordal, still watching over the parsonage and its residents.

The Johnsons, an Almont couple, recently translated the Sims church's early records from Norwegian to English. They learned that the

Sims congregation sent a letter to the bishop of their synod complaining about the paranormal activity in the parsonage and the resultant frequent loss of pastors. The bishop's response, if there was one, wasn't in the records.

Although some area residents say the Gray Lady has left her former home, volunteers who worked on the building in the summer of 2005 heard noises that sounded like footsteps coming from inside the parsonage while they camped outside. Now that the parsonage restoration is complete, perhaps Bertha Dordal is re-occupying her former first-floor bedroom in comfort.

The Glowing Church in Absaraka
Cass County

While you may be able to find Absaraka on a North Dakota highway map, you won't find it in the place index. Like so many small towns on the prairie, it was once a stop on a major railroad. Now it's now mostly a ghost town, with just a handful of residents. But unlike most ghost towns, Absaraka actually is said to be haunted.

The haunted building is the church. According to stories, the windows of this abandoned former Methodist church glow. They don't just glow, they glow with the shape of a cross. If you're able to look closely at any window, which is difficult as they've mostly been boarded up, you'll see the cross, and it moves with you if you go from side to side. Each side of the church has a window, and no matter which side you look from, you'll see the cross facing you.

Unfortunately, like so many haunting stories, this one has a rational explanation behind it, or at least some claim it does. The windows were evidently made with a cross design, and when the light from streetlights or moonlight hits them, the glowing cross appears inside. Sounds like a great explanation, doesn't it?

Despite that, there is one more story associated with it. A group of young people from Fargo decided to make the forty-five-mile trip to Absaraka one night. They came to the railroad tracks that cross the gravel road into the town, and the crossing lights started to flash. They looked down the tracks and saw the headlight of an oncoming train. They waited, but the train came no closer, and suddenly the headlight vanished. They went on into town, and were pretty creeped out at the sight of the church. When they drove back home and got out of their vehicle, they were even more frightened. Dozens of small handprints covered the back of their car. Were ghostly children trying to keep the curious teens away from their church? (Does this story sound just a little like an urban legend? Maybe you saw a movie like that once...)

The Lutheran Cemetery
Belfield

This is a short story about a small cemetery in a small town in western North Dakota. It seems that within the Lutheran Cemetery there is an old tree stump known locally as the Devil's Chair. Why the stump hasn't been removed from the cemetery is anyone's guess. But it seems that in the early 1980s, the cemetery was a happening party place, just far enough from town to avoid being busted by the cops or the county sheriff. One night, three young men each sat on the throne-like stump, and had their photos taken. Within the next month, each of them died – one while skiing, one in a car accident, and one, unusual given his young age, of a heart attack.

The story is often related among groups of young people who still party in the cemetery. These days, not many are willing to take the dare and sit in the Devil's Chair. Would you?

St. Patrick's Cemetery
Dickinson

The five nuns who died within a single week in 1926 at Dickinson's St. Joseph Hospital were buried side by side in St. Patrick's Cemetery, called St. Pat's by locals. Each day for the rest of her life, Sister Hildebrandis Flury, the sole survivor of the illness that had struck all six of them, visited their graves to pray for them. When she died in 1934, she was buried beside them.

St. Patrick's Cemetery with the graves of the deceased nuns

Since her death, it seems that Sister Hildebrandis continues to visit the graves of her sister nuns, usually shortly after sunset. Is it her spirit that roams the earth, stuck in the hospital she served and near the graves she tended? Or is it a residual haunting, like a film clip of the daily visits she made while alive, playing over and over? For the sake of Sister Hildebrandis, I hope it's the latter. She deserves to rest in peace, after all her years of service, and her years of loss.

The grave of Sister Hildebrandis in St. Pat's Cemetery.

Satan's Cemetery
Tagus

Tagus is a ghost town west of Minot, just over the county line into Mountrail County on old U.S. Highway 2. A railroad farm town founded in 1900, it was originally named Wallace, but apparently after some confusion with Wallace, Idaho, the residents changed the name to Tagus. A few people still live there, and it's still on the map, but most of the houses look abandoned.

The church no longer stands; it burned to the ground in 2001. The first theory for why it burned was an electrical problem, but careful examination revealed that the fire had been deliberately set. Tagus is too frequently the victim of vandalism, believed to be mostly from young people in Minot, although no one knows for sure. The cemetery is a mile or so outside the town, on a small hillside beside old Highway 2. The arch over the fenced entry reads "Tagus Cemetary." The cemetery, too, has been the victim of vandalism.

All of this began in the early 1970s. Minot, then the home of the Minot Strategic Air Command and still home to Minot Air Force Base, gained something of a reputation in North Dakota law enforcement circles as a drug town. It also had the reputation of being the center of a cult of Satanists. Author and journalist Maury Terry tied the drug culture and alleged Satanism in Minot to the Son of Sam murders in New York, and to a major crime ring around the country that recruited dealers and buyers through Satanism in his book, *The Ultimate Enemy*.

Although some of Terry's "facts" have been criticized as wild conspiracy theory, many area young people still believe that Satanists are active in the area. When the "Satanist" bar, the Falcon's Nest, in Minot was closed in the early 1970s, it was believed that the cult moved its activities to Tagus, where they would be less likely to be noticed. Those activities were said to center around the cemetery, where, it's said, beneath one tombstone is a stairway to an underground room where Satanic rituals are performed to this day. But be assured, there is no staircase in the Tagus Cemetery.

It does seem that some scent of evil hovers over Tagus. Once, a group of young people intending to visit the town at night stopped their car by the side of the road, and headed towards the town. Before they'd gone more than a few steps, they all began to feel violently ill, and two of them vomited before getting back to the car. They drove away and have vowed never to return. Others have driven through Tagus at night and claimed to see lights in buildings that are clearly abandoned.

Whether or not Tagus is a den of Satanism and haunting, one thing is certain: Its small population has had more than their fair share of vandalism. So if you visit Tagus and its cemetery, do so with respect for the decent people who still live there. Stay in your vehicle, and don't disturb their living or their dead. You never know what you might be stirring up.

A spooky abandoned house in haunted Tagus, North Dakota.

Old Main Hall, campus of NDSU in Fargo. *Photo courtesy of Nik Guse, Dakota Paranormal Investigators.*

College Haunts and Schoolyard Spooks

Colleges are the perfect spots for ghost stories to take root and grow. A story, once told, continues to be repeated to each incoming class, and like some twisted branch on an eldritch tree, changes and grows with each retelling. High schools aren't much different, although the stories don't always change as much. Nearly every college or university in North Dakota has at least one haunted building, and many of the high schools have their own ghostly tales.

North Dakota State University

Fargo

Two haunted halls grace the campus of NDSU. One of them, Ceres Hall, was the first women's dormitory to be built on what was then the North Dakota Agricultural College, around 1910. Prior to that, the women were housed in the Beale Dormitory on North 12th Street. Named for the goddess of agriculture, appropriate for the college, Ceres Hall is no longer a dormitory; it houses the Admissions Office, the Financial Aid Office, and several other administrative and management offices.

One popular story of the haunting of Ceres Hall goes back to the end of World War II, when, it is said, a man hanged himself from a pipe on the third floor, the main area of haunting. No actual ghost is mentioned in this story; just a feeling of being watched and the amorphous description, "weird happenings." The basement, in this same story, is another haunted area and feels more evil than the third floor, but again, no particular spirit is seen.

A second story of the haunting of Ceres Hall tells us that in addition to the hanged man, there was a girl – presumably a student residing in the hall – who, realizing that she was failing in all her courses, hanged herself from a pipe as well. Her spirit is said to be very active; she opens and closes doors and windows, and makes both banging and vocal noises at night.

In 2007, a Fargo-area paranormal research group investigated Ceres Hall. One of the investigators worked on the third floor. Although he saw a mysterious shadow and found a cold spot (though he neglected to mention how much colder that spot was from the rest of the area), he didn't see either the hanged man or student. A second investigator started in the basement area, where he saw a ball of red light, moved to the third floor where he found nothing, which he blamed on the security lighting, and then to the fourth floor, where he felt an aura of sorrow and a lost feeling. He attempted to provoke the spirits so he could capture EVPs (Electronic Voice Phenomena), but nothing happened.

The third investigator was mainly in the basement, where he found a strange cut-out in a brick wall. His photograph of this spot shows what appears to be a flame, and the group wonders if this might indicate a demonic entity. Despite the relative lack of results, the group felt that Ceres Hall is indeed haunted, and they hope to return for another investigation.

The other haunted building is Minard Hall. Construction began in 1902, and eventually Minard grew to a four-story building. It was originally the Science Hall. These days, it's home to the College of Arts, Humanities and Social Sciences. It also houses the Departments of Math and Psychology. Nearly every freshman and sophomore will attend at least one course, if not several, in Minard Hall.

The story told of the haunting of Minard has a few awkward moments. For example, it says the 4th story "attic" was built in 1901, but in fact it wasn't built until after 1903. However, the haunting dates to the 1920s, when that attic was said to have been used as a ballroom. After a particularly spirited dance party, two bodies were found the next morning by a janitor. Police felt it was a double homicide, but no suspects were found, much less arrested (and no newspaper stories about the double murder could be found, either). The story continues by saying that the fourth floor was closed in the 1960s because of the potential danger of rotting floorboards. Nevertheless, enterprising students have managed to sneak up to the attic in the dark of night and hold seances. Again, no particular spirits, not even those of the dead couple, have ever been spotted, but students who've been there note the eerie feeling of not being alone, and of being watched by a malevolent presence. As of yet, no paranormal investigation has occurred in Minard Hall.

Minard Hall, campus of NDSU. *Photo courtesy of Nik Guse, Dakota Paranormal Investigators.*

University of North Dakota
Grand Forks

The University of North Dakota in Grand Forks is blessed, or cursed, with three hauntings. The most famous, or perhaps infamous, is the ghostly co-ed who haunts the tunnels of the Wilkerson residence hall complex. Wilkerson is actually the dining hall, and was built around 1962. Over the next three years, five dormitories were built, connected to Wilkerson by a system of tunnels to protect students from the spring and fall heat and the frigid winters. According to most versions of the story, a young woman student was on her way to John C. West Hall late one night, and took a shortcut through the snow, past Wilkerson. In this version, by the way, the tunnels haven't yet been built. When she reached the dormitory, her key didn't work, so she waited outside the hall for help. In the icy Grand Forks night, she froze to death.

Now her spirit, usually seen legless and in a semi-transparent white nightshirt, haunts the tunnels, Wilkerson Hall itself, and the outside of West Hall. She is said to have short dark hair, and aside from her pallor and blue lips, is quite attractive. It's also said that when she's around, electronic devices, including cell phones, iPods, and televisions, blur with static until she's gone again.

Although many people who lived in the Wilkerson complex never heard the story, the few who did made sure it spread. It has made it into at least one ghost story book, and also onto several internet pages. One of these tells it in some detail, while another, purportedly written by a former student who was working the night shift at the Wilkerson Service Desk in 1988, is in great detail. He tells that two students appeared in front of him, wide-eyed, sweating, and shaking, and said that they'd seen "something" in the tunnel from West Hall. They led him back to where they'd been, and he too saw the Wilkerson ghost. He goes on to say that he found an old UND student newspaper article about the girl who froze to death in 1962, and that in further research with the Grand Forks Police Department, he found that they too have a record of her death. He took a copy of the newspaper article to the Housing Director, with whom he was friendly, and that individual said he'd heard the story before, always from Housing Authority employees, and that since there was nothing he could do about it, he (the Housing Director) hadn't taken it any higher up the UND chain of command.

There are a few problems with the story. First, West Hall was originally a men's dorm, not a women's dorm, so a girl wouldn't have been going there after 11 p.m. in 1962. Second, there are no recorded deaths of any student freezing to death in 1962 in available records, such as the Grand Forks Herald. The late news reporter, Chuck Bundlie, from Grand Forks's WDAZ TV investigated the story in the 1980s, and found no evidence to support it. It is an urban legend that probably grew out of the unbelievably cold winters, with bitter windchills that can reach -70 degrees or colder, in Grand Forks.

There may well be something paranormal in the Wilkerson tunnels, but it isn't a frozen girl from 1962.

Another hall at the University of North Dakota claimed to be haunted is Stacher Hall. In this classroom building, it's said that many students have seen a severed male arm on the second floor, out of a doorway to a graphics darkroom. This arm is said to appear throughout the year, and at any time of day or night. It's also said that a professor "conducted soundings" of the building and discovered aberrations that seemed to lead back to second floor darkrooms. Other eerie manifestations are a feeling of being watched by a malevolent presence, and the wafting of a woman's floral perfume on a breeze, in an air-conditioned building with no breezes to speak of.

There are problems with this story too, beginning with the building name. There isn't a Stacher Hall at UND. There is a Starcher Hall, which houses the biology department, and it's filled with equipment of all kinds relevant to biology and bio-chemistry—but somewhat lacking in darkrooms, and having no history of disembodied arms.

Or perhaps the tale-teller confused it with the Skalicky Technology Incubator, a relatively new building designed to support the early stages of tech-based entrepreneurial ventures. There are no reports of lonely arms seeking their owners at Skalicky Tech, however.

The final stop on the UND ghost tour is the Burtness Theatre. Burtness was UND's first home for the performing arts, and has a regular calendar of stage and studio productions. But, at least one student found the performance too spooky for his taste. He was given the keys so he could open the theatre for a show, but on entering the building, he was immediately overwhelmed by a sense of impending doom, and fled. When he told other students of his experience, several said that the building was haunted, and has been for years. Some students had even seen ghosts there. Others merely laughed. So is the Burtness Theatre haunted? There's no proof that it isn't, so maybe you should visit it for yourself!

Wilkerson Hall, campus of UND in Grand Forks. *Photo by Lorrie Hanson, courtesy of Night Light Paranormal Investigations.*

Valley City State University
Valley City

Valley City is a quiet small town on the Sheyenne River in eastern North Dakota. It seems an unlikely place for a haunting, but then, who can say where ghosts may choose to remain? Valley City State University has at least three possibly haunted buildings.

One of the haunted buildings is Snoyenbos Residence Hall. Although it's now a men's hall, according to the ghost story, it was once a women's dormitory. The story goes that a young woman who lived on the fourth floor became pregnant, but kept her pregnancy hidden. When she went into labor, she went into the woods along the river, and when her baby was born, she killed it and buried it there. The baby was later found, but the young woman was never seen again. At least, not alive. Her spirit haunts the fourth floor, specifically a bathroom and room 404. Filled with guilt, regret, and sorrow, she cries and moans on winter nights. Then again, it could be that North Dakota wind...

At least two other hauntings have been reported in Snoyenbos. One is a ghost on the third floor, although little is known (or said) other than that there's a ghost. Two screaming children yelling at each other disrupt the peace of the first floor, while another spirit turns on the lights quite regularly.

McFarland Hall is also said to have its own ghost. This ghost inhabits the third floor, where it paces back and forth late at night, perhaps reliving some wrong done to it when it was a living person. An executive assistant at the university president's office said that a night custodian had claimed to have heard strange noises at night in McFarland.

Finally, Vangstad Auditorium, the theater, is believed to be haunted. Martin Kelly, an associate professor of communication arts and director of theater has confirmed that there is a ghost story connected to the building, but said he knew none of the details. His daughter has written a play about the haunting, entitled "Gone," and the VCSU theater group plans to perform it. Doug Anderson, director of marketing and communications at the university, told a reporter that he "cannot confirm nor deny the presence of ghosts on the VCSU campus."

Ross Allison, of the Amateur Ghost Hunters of Seattle and Tacoma (AGHOST) visited Vangstad Auditorium to speak to VCSU students one October. He had time to do only a short tour of the campus, but did find that Vangstad had high EMF (electromagnetic field) readings, which can be an indicator of paranormal activity. An orb, or ball of light, was found in a picture taken of the stage in Vangstad, and another was found in a photograph from Snoeyenbos Hall.

Jamestown College

Jamestown

Jamestown college is a small, private co-educational school that was founded by Presbyterian settlers in 1883. The college spreads out over 110 acres in the beautiful James River Valley in southern North Dakota, west of Valley City. A Liberal Arts college, it is regularly ranked as one of the best of its kind in the country. Jamestown College offers over thirty different programs for baccalaureate degrees. Still affiliated with the Presbyterian church, it's generally a quiet, peaceful place of study. But that doesn't mean it's free of paranormal activity.

One commonly told story is of a student from the 1980s who lived in Kroeze Hall, a residence hall usually used for incoming freshmen that was built in 1957. This particular student had an obsessive-compulsive disorder, the story goes, that focused on his Rubik's Cube. He would spend hours turning rows of colors, the cube clicking incessantly. Understandably, his room-mate became upset with the constant annoyance, and one day when the student was at class, the room-mate took his cube and hid it.

The student returned to their room – D15 – and when he didn't see the Cube where he'd left it, he began to go mad. He tore the room apart searching for it, but couldn't find it. When the room-mate returned to the room, the student leaped on him and attacked him, tearing at the room-mate with his fingernails and attempting to bite him. A group of male students who heard the ruckus intervened, and held the student while one of them went to get Campus Security and an ambulance for the room-mate, who survived with few real injuries. After a psychiatric examination, the student was committed to the State Hospital, conveniently close to the College, and spent months there, performing the actions of manipulating a Rubik's Cube, but with empty hands. Eventually, deprived of the Cube and isolated at the hospital, the student killed himself.

Of course, that's not the end of the story. The spirit of the student is said to have returned to room D15 in Kroeze Hall, the place where he was happiest with his toy. At night, the unhappy occupants of the room can still hear the constant clicking of the cube. A true story or a college myth? Only those who have lived in Room D15 can answer that question!

Watson Hall is another haunted dorm. It's the oldest residence hall on campus, and like Kroeze is reserved for first-year students. In Watson Hall, a transparent little girl is said to walk the corridors of the second floor late at night. On the first floor, one particular room, never specified, apparently has poltergeist activity. Bottles and small objects fly off of shelves and desktops, posters are torn from walls, and the door opens and slams closed on its own. What happened to cause all this activity? One theory is that this room has a higher EMF level than other rooms in the building, and has become a nexus of energy from the hormonally-charged freshmen, and all that energy manifests as activity. There are no stories of tragedy for Watson Hall, so that's as good a theory as any, if indeed the haunting of Watson Hall is more than another urban legend.

Roosevelt School serves the children of Richardton
and possibly still serves the children of the past.

Haunted Schools Across the State

There are many stories of hauntings in elementary, middle, and high schools across the state, and many of them are very similar. Lockers that open and close, drownings in swimming pools, and bouncing basketballs are in most of them. But let's take a closer look.

The Factory

In Edgeley, a small town south of Jamestown on US Highway 281, an abandoned school house is now known as The Factory, although it was never used as one. The ghost of a child gazes out of one of the upstairs windows from dusk until just before dawn. The story is that she was accidentally stabbed with a pair of scissors by another child, and her lost spirit is now trapped in the school.

Argusville High School

The Argusville High School was abandoned several years ago, and now has a private owner, so trespassing there is illegal. That hasn't stopped young people from investigating on their own. Their reports include seeing ghostly figures and hearing laughter coming from unseen children. Others say that the building isn't haunted, and no one ever died there, although long ago a janitor had a heart attack in the boiler room.

Because of the many reports, the Argusville school was investigated by two paranormal investigation groups from the Fargo area, working together. They reported seeing shadow figures and unexplained lights, and hearing noises and voices. They were unable to capture anything on camera or video, but they did get several EVPs from different parts of the building. Some of them included, "Don't hate her" and "almost away." These investigators concluded that there was paranormal activity at the Argusville school, but not enough to label it "haunted."

Central and Magic City

The high school in Minot has two buildings, Central, for grades 9 and 10, and Magic City for grades 11 and 12. Central, built in 1910, is the older of the two buildings, and held all high school students until the 1970s when Magic City was born. The ghost story is from Central. According to the story, Central originally had a swimming pool, located under the risers of the theater. That area is understandably dark and forbidding. It's said that at the beginning of a school year, as part of the hazing of new freshman, a student was tied to a chair and thrown into the pool. Even then the pool was scarcely used, so the freshman, forgotten by his tormentors, drowned and wasn't found for about three days. After that incident, the pool was drained and closed off. Students still claim to hear screaming and splashing in the theater area at night, and sometimes wet footprints are found in the early morning. Both the dark pool and the three days for finding the body are common themes in this story and others, and they resonate with mythology from the distant past.

Standing Rock High School

Standing Rock High School is on the Standing Rock Sioux Reservation, south of Bismarck and on the west side of the Missouri River. It is haunted by a little boy who persecutes the cheerleaders. He runs back and forth during their practices, and occasionally shuts off the lights, leaving them in the center of the gymnasium, alone. It's also said that a janitor took some pictures of the lockers, and when they were developed, there was someone standing beside lockers 220 and 221 in the junior high area. Finally, the boys locker room is said to be haunted by a little boy – perhaps the same child who haunts the cheerleaders – and who can only be seen as a reflection in the locker room mirrors.

Horace Elementary School

The Horace Elementary School in the small town of Horace, south of West Fargo, is filled with footsteps in the night when the school is empty save for the person hearing them. Further, shadow people are said to roam the hallways at night, seen occasionally by janitorial staff or a teacher staying late.

Mandaree

Mandaree is on the Fort Berthold Reservation, which lies northwest of Bismarck and encompasses part of Lake Sakakawea. In the girls locker room of the high school there, voices are heard and sometimes shadowy or misty figures are seen. The sounds of footsteps and bouncing basketballs are also heard coming from the gym when it should be empty. Many of the residents of Fort Berthold feel that Mandaree is an evil area, filled with paranormal activity and haunted by witches, spirits and demons. The reason for the evil remains unexplained.

Anne Carlsen Center

In Jamestown, along with the State Hospital, a penitentiary, and Jamestown College, is a facility called the Anne Carlsen Center. Anne Carlsen was born with severe disabilities: she had no lower legs, and no forearms. She quotes her father, her inspiration, as telling her that what she did have was far more important than what she didn't: she still had her head, with curiosity, intellect, and a desire to learn. She overcame her handicaps, even learning to run, and went beyond high school to college, receiving a doctorate in education from the University of Minnesota. She then became the principal of the Good Samaritan School for Crippled Children, which had moved to Jamestown from Fargo, and eventually became its administrator, a post she held until her retirement in 1981. Even after that she stayed at the school as a consultant, mentor, and whatever the school needed, and in 1980, the school was renamed the Anne Carlsen Center for Children in her honor. It was later shortened to the Anne Carlsen Center. She passed away in 2002 at the age of 85.

The Center now provides services to people of all ages with severe disabilities and autism. It has dormitories, but is working on building a series of cottages, to provide the students with a more home-like feel, and assist in their reintroduction to their own homes and, eventually, jobs. But the school isn't an easy one for anyone. The ghost who allegedly haunts the Center is a sad one; a little girl with long blonde hair sits in the laundry room and just looks at the people who come in. It's obvious to those who see her that she isn't able to move, just as many of the students were immobile when they arrived at the Center. Perhaps instead of fearing her, those who see her should give her hope, show her how far they have come, and encourage her to move on to the better place where she belongs.

Belcourt
Belcourt is the main town of the Turtle Mountain Band of Chippewa Reservation, in Rolette county in north central North Dakota. Belcourt is named for an early French Catholic missionary, Father Belcourt, who built the first church and school in Belcourt. It is said that long ago there was a fire at the school in Belcourt that killed at least two people. Children now are said to see a man dressed in old raggedy clothes, with his hat in his hand, staring at the ground near the school and looking stunned. After the school was repaired, it was said that lights in the middle school restroom turn themselves off and on, but only when someone is in the restroom alone.

There actually was a fire at the middle school and the elementary school next to it on October 26, 1984, but there is no record of anyone dying as a result.

Shanley High School
Shanley High School is a private Catholic school in north Fargo that was built as the Sacred Heart Academy in 1889. It educates grades 9 through 12. The diocese decided to move the school to south Fargo, and over the summer of 2009, a new Shanley High was built, along with Sullivan Middle School, on land acquired by the diocese. The old high school building, which is slated to be turned into apartments, is said to be haunted. According to several sources, a variety of paranormal activity has been observed. Footsteps were heard by different teachers working late in a mostly-empty building. Each time, when they looked they found

no one in the hallways. An electrician working on air-conditioning equipment under the bleachers in the gym saw a figure in a hooded robe float through a brick wall, then float through the gym and through the wall on the other side. A woman on the janitorial staff working at night saw a girl walk out through a locked door, across the hall, and then through a picture of Mary on the opposite wall. It will be interesting to learn if activity continues, either in the new school or the apartments.

Fort Yates Community Grant School
The Fort Yates Community Grant School is located in the town of Fort Yates on the Standing Rock Sioux reservation. The school is reported to be haunted by the spirit of a little boy who was said to have been killed in the basement of the high school auditorium. He can be heard walking and running around the auditorium, and he's said to slam lockers and turn on showers in the boys locker room. His voice is sometimes heard in both places, although it's never clear what he's saying.

Lake Agassiz Elementary School
Bouncing basketballs appear again in Lake Agassiz Elementary School in Grand Forks. They're accompanied by the piano, which plays by itself, and the ghost of a giggling little boy. On the darker side, there are also said to be nauseating odors and a feeling of being watched along with a sense of impending doom in some of the darkened hallways. This is a school just crying out for an investigation.

West Fargo High
The high school in West Fargo apparently has a ghost in the auditorium. Known as Rupert, this spirit plays with the auditorium lights, turning them off and on and causing them to flicker. Some say he is the ghost of a janitor who fell from the high lights and broke his neck during the 1980s, although there is no record of a janitor's death in West Fargo High.

There are undoubtedly many more schools throughout the state who have haunting stories, with people falling, drowning, or being murdered, and their spirits remaining in the school. The high energy and vivid imaginations of children and the challenges of puberty are strong emotional forces, and can leave a mark even where no death has occurred. It may be that if a story is told often enough, it becomes the truth, even as it changes with each storyteller.

State Capitol Building, Bismarck

Haunted Government Buildings

The State Capitol Building

Bismarck

Long before Bismarck received its name, it was a small settlement on the Missouri River shoreline simply called the Crossing. It was the point where Indians had traditionally crossed the river, and white settlers did the same. In February of 1873, the city was named Edwinton, for a Northern Pacific railroad employee, and finally named Bismarck in July of 1873. Citizens and railroad entrepreneurs hoped the name would encourage Kaiser Wilhelm von Bismarck of Germany to invest in the community and the westward growth of the Northern Pacific Railroad, but no money was forthcoming.

In 1883, after fierce debate, the capitol of Dakota Territory was moved to Bismarck from Yankton, for 160 acres and $100,000. The move was also partly due to the desire of the Northern Pacific Railroad to have the capitol on its new line. In November 1889, North Dakota became a state, with Bismarck as its capitol. It was by then also the county seat of Burleigh County, organized in July of 1873, and named after Dr. Walter A. Burleigh, a prominent physician and entrepreneur.

But the Capitol Building you see today isn't the original. The first state Capitol building, a four-story red brick building in a mix of Romanesque and Classical Revival architecture, was constructed in 1884. It was met with mixed feelings. Many residents felt it looked out of place on the wide prairie, and it was well north of the edge of Bismarck at the time. Still, it was used first by the governor of Dakota Territory, then by the North Dakota state governor and legislature when the first legislative session convened after statehood in 1889.

Early in the morning of December 28, 1930, fire lit the sky north of town. The three-person fire department, along with citizens and government employees raced to the Capitol building to see flames pouring from the fourth story. Many of the employees entered the building to save valuable state papers and documents. Secretary of State Robert Byrne was able to get the original copy of the state's constitution, although he was injured in the process. State employee Jennie Ulsrud was burned trying to save some records from the State Treasurer's office. While the fires still burned, Governor George F. Shafer returned from St. Paul, where he'd been visiting.

As the Capitol burned and most of the state's documents were lost, the governor and a group of legislators and state officials discussed what they would do about the loss of important records as well as their own office space. Fortunately, no one was killed in the fire, although many of those trying to save documents suffered burns and smoke inhalation from their vain attempts to enter the building. The fire fighters soaked the smoldering ruins of the Capitol, then the nearby Liberty Memorial Building to keep it from catching fire as well. It was later learned that the fire was started when rags, varnish, and turpentine, kept by the janitorial staff to prepare for the next legislative session, apparently spontaneously combusted.

In the aftermath of the fire, government offices moved to the Liberty Memorial Building, and the governor's office was relocated to the Federal Building in downtown Bismarck. Discussions continued throughout 1931 about how much could be spent and what could be built to replace the devastated building. Finally, in 1932, ground was broken for the new building. Construction didn't go smoothly. At one point in 1933, workers, although considered lucky by state officials to have jobs at all in the midst of the depression, went on strike for better and safer working conditions and better pay. Governor William Langer declared martial law to break the strike, resulting in injuries and jail sentences for many workers, and construction continued.

The new building, consisting of a nineteen-story art deco tower housing the executive branch of government and a three-story wing housing the legislative branch, was finally completed in 1934. Employees working in the building after hours tell off-the-record stories of smelling smoke and hearing the screams of injured people, along with a rush of many footsteps. Evidently the fire repeats itself in spirit as a residual haunting, lest anyone forget those injured, or all that was lost.

The Liberty Memorial Building

The Liberty Memorial Building, completed in 1924, now houses only the State Library and Archives and the offices that go with them.

In earlier years, it was used for government offices, state trials, the State Historical Society, the State Museum, and the State Library. The basement level once contained the artifacts and materials not on the current display in the museum portion of the building, including, it's said, Indian skeletal remains. During that time, strange footsteps were heard, along with opening and closing doors, and voices calling out to employees. The source of these phenomena was nicknamed "the Stack Monster" because its seldom-seen shadowy figure roamed the stacks of books and artifacts in the sub-basement. The story of the events while those artifacts were there, one of the best known ghost stories in North Dakota, is covered at length in the book *Haunted America* by Michael Norman and the late Beth Scott.

It was hoped that the strange and spooky activity would end when the new Heritage Center opened in 1982, and all the artifacts were moved there. But in case the Stack Monster wanted to move with the materials, a special badge was made for him to reach the Heritage Center's storage areas; instead of a photo, it had a gray square. Most Library employees at the time felt the Monster, more a specter than a true monster, had left along with the bones blamed for his presence. One employee claimed to have seen a side door to the building open, and she believed that was the last they would see of the Monster.

These days, the basement stacks hold books, including those from the Federal Depository, and archived material from the many state departments. But paranormal activity continues. Several workers in the building have reported paranormal activity there, on condition of anonymity. The current State Librarian has allegedly threatened to fire anyone who talks about it to a journalist or a writer.

Apparently, books recently shelved reappear on the shelving carts when the library opens in the morning, and sometimes books left on carts are shelved when no one is there. Properly shelved books move by themselves to new locations, making searching for a book more difficult. Sometimes books fall off of shelves, and lights turn off or on when no one is near the switch. State Library employees still see the shadowy figure who roams the stacks both day and night. The figure is usually sighted at the far end of whatever row an employee is looking down, and then is seen to duck quickly out of sight. And there is no reported paranormal activity with the artifacts that were transferred to the North Dakota Heritage Center.

In the spring of 2010, the State Library had some rewiring done by an outside contractor. They worked at night in the ground floor (basement, from the front) and sub-basement for several weeks. One morning one of the workers was leaving just as a Library staff member arrived. She reported that the hair on his arms was standing up, and he looked shaken. He asked her if the building still had a ghost. When she shrugged in response, he said, in effect, that no amount of money would be enough to make him spend another night in the library's sub-basement. Pale and shaking, he fled the basement.

Whatever this phantom is, it may have made Liberty Memorial Building's basement its permanent home.

Liberty Memorial Building, on the Capitol Mall, Bismarck.

Public Library
Harvey

Another well-known haunting in North Dakota is in the Public Library in Harvey. The story has appeared in books and in several newspapers across the state, most often around Halloween. But this isn't an old legend; this is an on-going haunt.

It did start long ago, in October of 1931, when young Sophie Eberlein, who lived with her second husband in Harvey, was gruesomely murdered by that husband. Their house was exactly where the Public Library now stands. And the room in which Sophie was bludgeoned to death? It was exactly where library director Marlene Ripplinger's office is now located.

Ms. Ripplinger and other librarians don't much like to talk about it, especially around the October anniversary of Sophie's murder, and as winter progresses and the nights get long, dark, and cold. But they will talk, if pressed. She'll tell about keys and books that disappear, then reappear somewhere else, or, as if to taunt them, exactly where they were before they vanished. Once a filled book cart was moved so that it blocked an inside door in the library. It took two people to push the door open, and they both knew that no one could have gotten out of that room with the filled cart in front of the door.

The indications of a haunting started soon after the building was completed, around 1989 or 1990. Lights started flickering off and on. Ms. Ripplinger and others were confused by this; the building was new, the wiring was new, so there shouldn't be a problem. Electricians were called in, and they found no reason for it, but the flickering continued. When other things began to happen, like the moving of small objects, and the occasional opening and closing of doors, and even the locking and unlocking of doors when no one was in the building, they knew that something was going on. One of the librarians checked the building site's history, and learned about Sophie, and since then, the oddities have been attributed to her.

One of Marlene Ripplinger's favorite stories of Sophie's activity, which she tells with the practice of one who has told it many times before, is about a book she used to use for weekly story time for the children who came to the library. It was a colorful book, and she always left in the same place on the shelves. One day it wasn't there. Ripplinger and the other librarians searched the library for weeks, going to the length of removing all the books from the shelves. They finally gave up, and Marlene assumed that the book had been stolen or thrown away.

Several weeks later, Marlene came into the library one morning, and there was the book, right where it had always been kept. She was stunned. She admitted in an October 30, 2009, interview with the *Fargo Forum*, "I think she [Sophie] messes with our minds."

She says that often the keys they need to lock up the library vanish just at closing time. They'll search the library, look at all the places they've been, then say, "'Okay, Sophie, I need to get home now.' And all of a sudden, there are the keys." Now it could be just forgetfulness – but it could be something paranormal.

Ms. Ripplinger told the Forum about a woman who visited the library a few years ago, and brought in a bunch of what looked like family heirlooms. The woman said that they belonged to the family of her first husband, a family from the Harvey area, and she felt that if they had historical importance they belonged in Harvey. A librarian asked her who her first husband's family was, and was astonished when the woman explained that her first husband was Sophie Eberlein's grandson. The woman said that her first husband's family never talked about the murder, and the librarian told her about the strange things that happened in the library, and both women wanted to know more.

Then the woman's husband came in, and his expression changed as he told them that he felt a presence in the library that wasn't fond of men. Ms. Ripplinger said that the hair on the man's arm stood up. He suggested that they cleanse the library of Sophie's spirit, and gave her some instructions on helping Sophie "go to the light." Ripplinger hasn't tried that yet, but if you happen to visit Harvey, and stop in at the library and talk to them, they may just let you try it.

County Courthouse
Eastern North Dakota

In a quiet county in eastern North Dakota, there's a county courthouse with strange activity. The county authorities don't want a host of ghost-seeking visitors, so the county and the courthouse location will have to remain anonymous.

Some of the reported activity includes cold spots, whispering voices, doors opening and closing on their own, chairs moving by themselves, and a feeling of being watched in some rooms in the building. Although the building has a long history, and no doubt more than one person was convicted in the various courtrooms, no one is known to have died there.

A paranormal investigation was done in the building by a group from Fargo, who in this instance will also remain anonymous. The investigators, on two separate trips, recorded multiple EVPs, and found abnormally high EMF (electromagnetic field) readings in a cold spot that was shown by their thermal equipment to be several degrees colder than the surrounding temperature. There was nothing electrical in that area to account for either the EMF readings or the cold temperature. One of the theories about cold spots is that spirits require energy to manifest themselves. If there isn't a source of energy nearby, they'll take it from the surrounding air, creating a cold spot.

They used both digital and analog EMF detectors, as wells as K-2 EMF meters, whose readings show the level of electromagnetic energy by the number of lights on the end of the device that light up. One theory of ghost-hunting is that if there is no natural reason for electromagnetic energy, like exposed wiring or poor electrical connections, high consumption electrical equipment like computers or even microwave ovens, then a high EMF reading may indicate the presence of a spirit or other entity. Yet another theory is that high electromagnetic energy acts like a battery charger for ghosts, so they are drawn to areas with high EMF. K-2 meters are often used to attempt communication with entities; they are asked to light up the lights if their response to a question spoken by an investigator is "yes" or "no."

Two EVPs in the courthouse, taken at different times, had the same message. One said "help" and was actually heard by the investigators, so isn't truly an EMF, although it appeared on the audio recording as well. The other said what sounded like "help me." Hearing the words in an EVP is somewhat subjective; it may not sound to one person like it does to another. But both these EVPs were remarkably clear, and there was no disagreement among the investigators as to what was said.

Does this mean the courthouse is haunted? The investigators will tell you that at this point, they will verify there is paranormal activity, but not enough that they can confirm there is an actual haunting. They do plan to do another investigation, and no one can say what evidence they will find in that one.

Haunted Businesses and Spirited Stores

There are plenty of haunted restaurants, hotels, stores, and even theaters scattered around the state, or at least there are plenty that are said to be haunted. Some of the hauntings are scary, some sad, and some, well, some are just interesting, and make you wish you'd been there long ago. Follow me through some haunted hotels, cafes, stores, and a very creepy camp!

Peacock Alley and the Patterson Hotel
Bismarck

Peacock Alley is a happening bar and restaurant in Bismarck, on the corner of 5th Street and Main Avenue in the heart of Bismarck's downtown district. The business is on the ground floor of what was the Patterson Hotel, but was redone and became assisted living apartments for seniors. Before it was the Patterson, this building was the Hotel McKenzie, built in 1910. Alexander McKenzie, the owner, was a famous, or perhaps an infamous, political figure in Bismarck and state politics.

McKenzie was also a friend of William Langer, twice governor of the state and something of a shady character himself, earning the name "Wild Bill" as federal agents pursued him on a charge of illegal liquor smuggling. The Hotel McKenzie was the site of many political meetings where under-the-table deals and decisions were made.

According to those who still remember, some pretty wild parties and dances were held on the rooftop garden, which offered a view of all of Bismarck. In 1910, the seven-story hotel was the tallest building in the state. It lost that honor to the Capitol in the 1930s. In 1940, it was sold to Edward G. Patterson, former manager of the Northwest Hotel in Bismarck, and it remained a hotel until the remodel in the 1970s.

Patterson Place Apartments, once the Hotel McKenzie, and Peacock Alley. Downtown Bismarck.

The beautiful and intricate scrollwork on the outside of the restaurant and bar entrances was the inspiration for the name "Peacock Alley." The restaurant is famous, among other things, for its beer-batter buns, and its first-class steak, seafood, and service. The bar is frequented mainly by downtown workers and businessmen, with the requisite big-screen TVs tuned to sports programs, and is the perfect place for a quick lunch on weekdays.

Behind that lovely, and tasty, front, there lurks a haunted hotel. Visitors to the Patterson Hotel often complained to the manager about loud conversations and arguments, that always seemed to be held in empty rooms. Those staying on the seventh floor complained about dance bands playing above them, along with noisy party-goers, on quiet week nights when no bands or parties were scheduled.

These days, staff in Peacock Alley may tell you, if you agree not to reveal their names, their own stories of hauntings. It seems that some nights, when the bar is closed for the night and all the glasses are neatly hanging in the rack over the bartender's station, someone moves the clean glasses onto the bar, and sometimes onto the tables around it. In the restaurant, silverware is rearranged, and napkins are pulled from water glasses and spread out on the table. In the kitchen, pots and pans are rearranged after everyone has gone home for the night, and occasionally a knife goes missing, only to turn up within a couple of days. Wait staff have reported cold spots, and one young woman says that she was touched on the arm while waiting to get an order from the kitchen and no one was around her.

It seems like the politicking, partying days of McKenzie and Langer linger at Peacock Alley, although they seem to have left the Patterson Place apartments. No one feels that their presence is malevolent or dangerous, but most admit that it can be pretty creepy, especially after dark. And most of the staff would rather not stay there after closing. Would you?

A Prairie Bed and Breakfast
Central North Dakota

North Dakota's "prairie pothole" region, about an hour's drive southeast of Minot describes a landscape of rolling prairie dotted with ponds and wetlands that provides a wonderful habitat for migratory birds as well as other types of wildlife. This is a truly lovely part of North Dakota, and is often overlooked by both tourists and North Dakota residents. It's also called the Lake and Garden region. Here you will find a charming

B&B owned by a city couple who had always dreamed of owning and operating a bed and breakfast. They ended up with much more.

The historic building they bought was a former rural 10,000-square-foot building that used wind power for electricity and had indoor plumbing along with a lovely variety of rooms. They were able to turn the building into a comfy and cozy bed and breakfast with three unique rooms with bathrooms en suite; and the restaurant portion serves not just breakfast, but also lunch and dinner.

But just like with other buildings, the remodeling that made this wonderful inn great triggered a haunting. According to the stories, a fire in the building's past killed a young boy and a cigar-smoking man, and the remodelers smelled smoke from both the fire and the cigar in the basement. Other alleged paranormal activity included the sounds of moaning heard at night, small objects being moved around when no one was there to move them, lights flickering on and off, and cold spots throughout the building.

You probably won't find any cold spots at the B&B, nor are you likely to smell smoke, because now you will find the Inn to be a non-smoking retreat (for all humans at least). If you want to smoke, you'd be smart to do it outside—not just because of the management, but you wouldn't want to upstage the resident ghosts.

The Rock Roof Inn
Glen Ullin

Glen Ullin is located in western North Dakota, just south of Interstate 94 about halfway between Bismarck and Dickinson. The town may be fairly small, but the hospitality is huge, and the country around it is both beautiful to look at and excellent for bird hunting.

The Rock Roof Inn is a Bed and Breakfast that has five beautifully decorated rooms for travellers and hunters (and a kennel if you bring your hunting dog). It began life as a small farmhouse, but when owners Pat and Margaret Swift redecorated the house, it tripled in size and is now a delightfully cozy inn. Pat is a retired rancher and farmer, and is happy to escort hunting parties, while Margaret is an award-winning artist who loves to cook and bake. Her studio is part of the Inn, and besides her on-going work, it has arts and crafts and other products from North Dakotans for sale.

It's pretty much guaranteed that anyone who stays there won't go away hungry after one of Margaret's breakfasts. Her artistry with paint is nearly matched by her hand with caramel rolls, sour-cream twists, and oatmeal/buttermilk muffins, which complete a hearty breakfast of eggs and locally made sausage, or whatever she chooses to make. It's also usually a guarantee that visitors will get a good night's sleep.

Two recent visitors, though, family members travelling together, had an interesting experience. After locking the door and turning off the cable television and the lights, they both went to sleep. A couple of hours later, the older woman asked the younger to close the door. The younger, thinking her relative was talking in her sleep, said that she would, but didn't bother getting out of bed, since she knew she'd locked the door. A little while later, the older woman again asked her to close the door. This time the younger woman sat up, and realized that the room was lighter than it should be, then saw that the light was coming in through the opened door. She swears she locked the door, and said that as she got up to close and lock it again, she felt a presence, although the presence didn't frighten her.

Perhaps it was Pat's father, Ray, who built the original house, checking out the strangers in his home. Or maybe she actually forgot to close the door, and it opened on its own. Most visitors describe a pleasant, comfortable stay with no paranormal reports.

The Rough Riders Hotel
Medora

Medora, in southwestern North Dakota, is a popular tourist spot in the summer; in fact, it may be North Dakota's most popular tourist destination. The town began as scruffy Little Missouri (Little Misery to those who lived there) in the 1870s, but became the town of Medora in 1883, after the arrival of the Marquis de Mores and Theodore Roosevelt. The town grew as ranches in the area, and the Marquis's slaughterhouse, packing plant and shipping operation grew, and in 1884 and 1885, a hotel called the Metropolitan was built by businessman George Fitzgerald. Looking at all of the businesses planned by the Marquis, Fitzgerald expected a boom town, and it was for a while.

In 1903, the hotel's name was changed to the Rough Riders Hotel, honoring Theodore Roosevelt's Rough Riders and their valor in the Spanish American War. The year 1903 also marked the first time that Roosevelt visited North Dakota as the President of the United States – and as the first President to visit Medora.

Since that time, the hotel has been operated by many different families as a bar and restaurant with upstairs sleeping rooms for visitors or people passing through, but it was gradually falling apart. The hotel underwent a major renovation and reconstruction when Harold Schafer and his business, the Gold Seal Company of Bismarck, bought the restaurant and other businesses in Medora. In July of 1965, the Rough Riders Hotel opened for business again, with a new restaurant and bar and renovated hotel rooms on the second floor. Schafer founded the Theodore Roosevelt Medora Foundation, a non-profit organization to own and operate the businesses he had purchased, after he sold Gold Seal. By 2008, it was obvious that the hotel needed more renovation, and more rooms. The original structure was completely renovated before the 2009 tourist season (basically Memorial Day to Labor Day), and the dining room and bar were expanded during the summer. Historic items and photos from Medora's past decorate the dining room, and a fireplace was built with bricks salvaged from the original Capitol building. Expansion of the hotel is in progress. Sixty-eight new rooms and a conference center will be completed in 2010.

For many years, performers in the Medora Musical along with many other seasonal workers lived for the summer in the hotel. Rumors of old hauntings were rampant for a time, with ghostly cowboys walking the second floor, a young boy haunting the roof, and toilets flushing by themselves. The veracity of these stories is debatable, but it is true that Medora is a small town with a big history, and if nothing else, the wild and woolly past lingers in the dusty streets of this little town in the Badlands.

Apple Creek Country Club
Bismarck

East of Bismarck on Old Highway 10 is Apple Creek Country Club, Bismarck's first private golf course and dining club. In the 1960s and 1970s, the food at Apple Creek was said to be the best in town, and the golf course had no real rival. Employees of Apple Creek's restaurant, which was open all year long, tended to stay and become fixtures.

Some people say that things changed in the 1990s after the death of a favorite waitress and a member of the cleaning crew. It seems that they may not have wanted to leave their jobs, even after death. When employees have stayed late, they often hear footsteps in empty rooms. When the kitchen staff arrives to start lunch, the smell of cooking is sometimes waiting for them in the kitchen. Occasionally tables are found set, when they'd been cleared the night before, and dirty dishes arrive in the kitchen when no one remembers taking them there.

Are these stories true, or merely another campfire story, to spook the new employees? Members of the country club haven't noticed anything out of the ordinary, at least not that they'd talk about, but it may just be possible that their favorite waitress is still serving them.

Georgia's and The Owl
Amidon

Sleepy little Amidon, a town of about thirty in southwestern North Dakota, is the smallest town to be a county seat in the state. It also boasts one of the better restaurants in the state. Georgia's and the Owl serves lunch and dinner daily, and has a nicely varied menu. But some people visit for the paranormal action.

Georgia's and the Owl and Amidon.

Stories say that the spirit of an active young boy haunts the restaurant. This spirit races around and occasionally bumps into diners and waitresses. Sometimes he pulls the single-serve bags of potato and corn chips off of their rack and scatters them onto the floor, where they're found the next day. It's also said that the restaurant was investigated by a team of paranormal investigators, who caught some EVPs with men's and women's voices, although apparently none of them were clear enough to tell what was said.

The White House

Medora

This beautiful building in Medora used to be a private home, but is now a store with unique clothing and accessories. In its days as a home, the owners experienced strange things, like cupboard doors opening and closing by themselves, and lights turning themselves on and off. Windows and doors also opened themselves. Finally the owner sold the house.

The new owners turned the house into a store. Since the remodeling was completed, they say that no paranormal activity has occurred. Why things happened with the first owners is unknown; there are no accounts of deaths or traumatic activity in the history of the building. A psychic/medium said that it was possible that a mischievous entity had attached itself to the previous owner; this wouldn't be anything that would harm them, just something that would play little tricks on them. Even playful little tricks can get old, though.

The White House Store, Medora.

Home Sweet Home
Minot

This architecturally interesting Victorian building in Minot, said to date from 1894, was originally a private home. Very little is known about the home's owners over the years, and much of what is told may not be true. One story says that a man hanged himself in the upper level of the tower, or attic. Another story of a more recent date says that a homeless man had been drinking and sleeping in the parking lot behind the store and next to the river. He got up in the night, the story goes, and fell into the river and drowned. Now, of course, both of these men are said to haunt the building.

Home Sweet Home, Minot.

Inside the building are antiques, collectibles, candles, baby clothes, and a range of "Pride of Dakota" products. Free coffee or tea, along with samples of cookies, are offered to patrons. The rooms are small, and there are frequent steps up or down. Although one of the haunting stories talks about candy being moved from one dusty jar to another, there are no longer any jars of candy on display. The door to the upper levels is usually locked, probably because it's used for storage. Although there are stories of cold spots in the attic, the icy North Dakota winter winds could account for most of those.

The drowned ghost is said to appear in the river at precisely 4:39 a.m. To date, no one has been able to see or photograph this ghost. Maybe the morning hours are just too early for ghost hunters!

If you visit Minot and want to find a special gift for yourself or someone else, Home Sweet Home is a great place to visit. If you're looking for a ghost, though, you may need to search someplace else (or get up very early).

Barber Auditorium

Marmarth

From a distance, Marmarth may look like a ghost town, but it's still inhabited by about 150 people. Marmarth was founded in 1907 when the Milwaukee Railroad was built through the area, and by 1915 had a population of over 100 people, along with a fully operational electric light plant. The town was named for Margaret Martha Fitch, the daughter of the Milwaukee Railroad President.

Today, the town still has a bank, a beauty shop, and a restaurant and bar, along with the Bunkhouse, which is sort of a motel, except that the bathroom is down the hall and shared. It's a building from the early 1900s, and has never been remodeled, which explains why it's not a luxury hotel. Marmarth also offers fossil digs, a shady spot beneath the cottonwoods along the Little Missouri River, and some fascinating buildings.

The Mystic Theatre, listed on the National Register of Historic Places, belongs to the Marmarth Historical Society and has annual Cowboy Poetry gatherings as well as live theater with local talent. But for architecture and haunts, it's outdone by the Barber Auditorium. The Auditorium was built in 1909. The ground floor housed businesses, including a bank, and the upper floor was the Opera House, which in its day was the finest playhouse west of Minneapolis. The Barber building burned in 1918 but was promptly rebuilt. These days, the building has

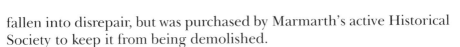

fallen into disrepair, but was purchased by Marmarth's active Historical Society to keep it from being demolished.

Most of the Barber Auditorium's upper level isn't safe, but those few who have ventured there at night say there is a shadowy figure of a man who sits in a seat as if watching a play. Murmured words and faint haunting music are said to come from the stage area at night, and one former soprano is determined that the show will go on, and tries to open the curtains from time to time. Are these stories true? Most historians say they aren't, any more than the story that people staying in the Bunkhouse have heard the Medora to Deadwood stage rumble past in the middle of the night. But you might want to take a trip down to Marmarth on a nice spring day and see for yourself. Remember that the Auditorium is private property, and be sure to get permission before you attempt to enter it.

Trollwood Park

Fargo

Trollwood Park was once the home of the Trollwood School for the Performing Arts, and in the summer, concerts were held there regularly. Some Fargo residents used to see the ghost of a woman dancing around the trees during concerts. It's also said that a pauper's grave yard was inside the Park's boundaries, and that three little graves had markers.

Sadly, the Red River flood of 2009 destroyed much of Trollwood Park. The school has been relocated, and the concerts are held elsewhere. Has the ghostly woman followed the performers, or does she still dance among the toppled trees of Trollwood? Unless the Park is restored, no one may ever know.

Camp Mondak

near Dunseith

In northern North Dakota, north of Dunseith and east of St. John on ND Highway 43, near Carpenter Lake, there was a camp called Camp Mondak. The haunting story goes like this: Camp Mondak was a place for troubled youth, sort of a summer reform school camp. One summer in the 1950s, five of the boys got together and killed the counselors. One boy felt remorseful and hanged himself from one of the trees. If you visit the camp at night, you might see his transparent body hanging from a tree, and you'll hear the crazy laughter of the murderers and the screams of their victims.

The real story is that the camp was home to a program called "Lighthouse of Hope," a group home for juveniles run by a religious group. On a summer afternoon, a boy named Darrell Wayne Red Paint decided to run away, and convinced another boy, Daniel C. DeNoyer, to go with him. They went to the farm of Donald and Bernice Johnson, an elderly couple whose home was near the camp. Darrell shot the Johnsons with their own shotgun, and he took their car. He and Daniel drove to the home of Daniel's girlfriend in nearby St. John.

When the camp's director, Franklin Bell, realized that the boys were missing, he called the Rolette County Sheriff's office to tell them. Later a deputy called Bell to tell him about the Johnsons' murders, and their suspicion that the boys may have been involved in it. Later that evening, the mother of Daniel's girlfriend called Bell to let him know that the two boys were there. The boys agreed to turn themselves in to the sheriff if Bell would take them in. Bell drove to St. John to pick them up, and within a few minutes of picking the boys up, his car was pulled over by a deputy who'd been following him, who then arrested the boys. Bell followed them to the county jail in Rolla, and when they got there, Bell asked if he could speak to Darrell privately. In their conversation, Darrell admitted to Bell, a former state highway patrolman, that he had shot the Johnsons. Bell advised him to ask for an attorney before admitting anything to the sheriff.

Darrell was convicted of two counts of murders, and sentenced to two life terms in the State Penitentiary in Bismarck, where he remains. Daniel was tried as a juvenile, and his records are sealed.

Visitors to the site of the former Camp Mondak will probably find what they are looking for. If they don't know the history and are looking for a peaceful place in the birch trees near a lake, with a summer wind whispering through the leaves, they'll find it. If those familiar with the story search for the unholy residue of a double murder, they may find just that. Camp Mondak was forced to close after the Johnsons were killed; the remaining boys at the camp were transferred to other facilities. The land is privately owned, and "No Trespassing" signs block the narrow gravel road. You may be prosecuted if you decide to ignore the signs, and you just might be terrified as well.

Haunted
Roads and Bridges

Given that North Dakota is a large state with a small population and an abundance of roads, it's hardly surprising that some of them are haunted. Roads, whether they are Interstate Highways or paths through a dark forest, lead the traveler from one place to another. The places aren't always physical; a haunted highway can lead a traveler from his known safe world of reality to a place where the previously unknown and unseen make their appearance. That journey may even lead to inner growth.

Sitting Bull Bridge, Mandan.

Bridges have even more psychological, or maybe mythological, implications. They cross a danger, a dark underpass or a raging river, and they connect two discrete places to each other. Yet while the traveler is on the bridge, he is neither here nor there, for the bridge is a dangerous place of its own, and may have a life of its own.

The Original Memorial Bridge

A railroad bridge was built across the Missouri between Bismarck and Mandan in 1882, but early drivers had to use a ferry or winter ice to cross the river until 1922, when the Veterans Memorial Bridge was built on what was then Highway 10, and now Old Highway 10 or "the Strip." People driving across the bridge, a humpback truss style bridge, heard a whining noise from the surface of the road until it was resurfaced with asphalt in the 1990s.

While most drivers thought nothing of it, some who heard the sounds late at night swore they were the howls and cries of men who died during construction. There are no records of construction deaths, but the legend continued until a wider, safer replacement for the narrow old bridge was completed in 2008. When construction was completed, the original bridge was imploded, its rubble removed from the river and placed in a landfill, and the new bridge is quiet again.

Four Bears Bridge

The first Four Bears Bridge crossed the Missouri River on land belonging to the Fort Berthold Reservation, home to the Three Affiliated Tribes, the Mandan, Hidatsa, and Arikara. It was built in 1934, and was only the fourth bridge in the state to cross the Missouri. In 1943, the river flooded badly, covering all the bridges then in existence, and the U.S. Congress ordered the Army Corps of Engineers to look into, and develop, plans for flood control along the Missouri.

When a plan was approved, it involved the building of a series of dams down the length of the river. Garrison Dam would flood the valleys where the three tribes had farmed for hundreds of years, and the people were forced by the government to give up their farms and move to higher ground. A new town, creatively named New Town, was built on what would be the shore of the reservoir created by the new dam, and Elbowood, where the bridge had stood, would be under the waters of Lake Sakakawea.

The Four Bears Bridge, however, was seen as still useful, because its construction style wouldn't require piers to be built all the way to the lake bottom. While the dam was being built, piers were put in place at New Town and across the river, along with long sections of deck truss. When the water was finally high enough, Four Bears Bridge was floated upriver for forty miles and attached to the piers and trusses. When completed, it was 4,438 feet long – almost a mile – and 20 feet wide. When the lake was at its projected highest water level, the bridge would be about 44 feet above the water.

As you can imagine, many of the people of Fort Berthold were greatly unhappy at the loss of their land, and their forced move to New Town. Although the bridge was, at its heart, the same bridge that had crossed the Missouri River at Elbowood, and that should have helped keep a spiritual connection with the former location, trust in the bridge had faded. The trusses that connected the old bridge to the new shorelines were very long, and had the appearance, at least, of being poorly supported. But the bridge continued to be used by car and truck traffic, until that traffic increased in the 1990s when a casino was built at New Town, and all the new traffic began to take its toll on the aging bridge.

The state finally decided that a new bridge was necessary, and to incorporate the views and desires of the Three Affiliated Tribes, a group called the Cultural Advisory Committee, or CAC, was formed to help develop the final appearance of the new bridge. After much debate among the parties involved in bridge construction, which included the CAC, tribal representatives, the engineering firm that was preparing the structural design, city and county representatives, the Federal Highway Administration, and the State Historical Society, a basic structural design was approved, and it was decided that the CAC would choose the tribal symbols to be used in the final exterior sides of the bridge and along the pedestrian walkway.

Construction began in April of 2003, and given the size and cost of the project (4500 feet, and $55 million), it proceeded fairly smoothly, although some of the elders in the area believed that despite the recognition given to the two chiefs named Four Bears who gave the bridge its name, and the cultural symbols of each of the three tribes that would decorate the completed project, the new bridge was cursed. Cursed, perhaps, by those who had lost their homes when Garrison Dam was completed and flooded tribal lands, or cursed by those who came before, whose graves now lay under hundreds of feet of water. Whatever the case, in June of 2003, the bridge claimed its first victim, a worker from Texas who was struck by a track that separated from a crane and fell to the ground. He was seriously injured, and although at the time, hospital officials said that with physical therapy he could recover completely, he never returned to work at the bridge.

The next major incident came on December 1, 2004, when a steel support structure that was being assembled on the bridge suddenly collapsed. One man was killed instantly, and three others were seriously injured. Two of them had been working near the top, and were rescued from where they hung upside down in their safety harnesses. Whispers about the curse that had begun before construction, were now spoken out loud. Work on the bridge stopped and an investigator from the Occupational Safety and Health Administration arrived the next day. Representatives of the construction company also sought to find the cause of the collapse. No reason was ever found.

The bridge opened to traffic in September of 2005, and a three day purification and dedication ceremony was held in October of that year. Two small pieces of the original bridge were kept and are displayed in the parking lot of the casino. They can still be seen there. People still wonder about the curse, and if the blood of the injured men, and the dead worker, will color the future of the Four Bears Bridge. And if you drive there on a dark December night, look up from time to time; they say that although the hanging men weren't killed, their spirits appear, hanging above the bridge in the icy night air.

Lost Bridge Near Killdeer

In the early 1930s, a bridge was built across the Little Missouri River, about twenty miles north of Killdeer on State Highway 22. It took another twenty years to build the road from Killdeer to the bridge, which accounts for the name of the bridge, which for those years was a bridge to – nowhere. Time and usage caught up with the bridge, and it was dismantled and replaced in 1994. A piece of the bridge, along with a memorial plaque, sit near the new bridge in memory of the past.

Very near the bridge is the site of 1864's Battle of Killdeer Mountains. General Sully led his troops to the Killdeer Mountains against the Lakota (Sioux) to get revenge for the Minnesota Massacre two years previously, in which a band of Lakota warriors attacked a small town in Minnesota. It wasn't the Killdeer band, but that hardly mattered, as feelings were running high in the new towns and farmsteads. Two of Sully's 3,000 men were killed, but over 100 of the poorly armed and unsuspecting Lakota died in the battle, and more died over the next few weeks, as Sully's troops scoured the Badlands, looking for any who had escaped the battle.

According to locals, a black dog with red eyes sometimes stands on the bridge at night. Black dogs have an association with the devil in folklore. This particular dog sometimes turns into a man clothed completely in black, including a black hat and drover-style coat; he also flaunts hooves instead of boots!

Killdeer, and the Lost Bridge, are just south of the Fort Berthold Reservation. Although it's not a Lakota Reservation, it is filled with stories of sightings of witches and devils. Is the black dog/man a devil or a demon? Or is it the spirit of a Lakota warrior in modern garb, still hoping to avenge his death? No one is sure, but everyone in the area says that Lost Bridge is not a place you want to get a flat tire or have your car break down, especially after dark.

Old Lady Black Tongue

You won't find Black Tongue Hill on any map, but residents of Fort Yates, on the Standing Rock Sioux Reservation, can tell you that it's on State Highway 24, about fifteen miles south of Fort Yates. Many years ago – and no one seems quite certain how many – a woman named Old Lady Black Tongue lived on that hill. "Old Lady" shouldn't be considered derogatory; it's actually a term of respect, indicating that this woman was an elder with wisdom and dignity. But her life was ended when she was struck by a car while walking along the road.

No one knew who ran her down, either, but apparently Old Lady Black Tongue is still looking for him. She is said to walk along the road at night, wearing a long black dress and a black shawl, and when a car passes, she will walk or run to keep up with it, so she can look into the windows and see if it's the driver who killed her. After a few minutes, she disappears. Although if her killer should drive that road again, she might not be as forgiving to him as she is to the innocent drivers of today.

The Lady In White

Just as there's a woman in black on one road, there's a lady in white on another. The road she haunts is said to be between Leroy and Akra, but nothing remains of either town, on paper or on a map, so it's any-body's guess where this road actually is. Seriously, it's supposed to be near Minot, in the Souris Valley and the prairie pothole region of North Dakota. There is a bridge over a swampy area along the road.

Two stories are told of who the spirit is. One says that she was married to a soldier fighting in World War II, and when she received the telegram notifying her of his death, she took a rope to the bridge and hanged herself. Those who tell this story say they have seen a young woman in a flowing white dress, with a noose around her neck, standing on the bridge.

The other story says that she was the daughter of an area farmer and was induced to go for a walk by a traveling salesman. When they reached the bridge, he made a move on her. Being a good girl, she spurned his advances. Instead of letting her go, he strangled her and threw her body into the swamp. Now, she may appear, in her long white dress, standing on the road on either side of the bridge or on the bridge itself, and she looks with glowing eyes into the windows of each car that passes in the night. Like Old Lady Black Tongue, she is trying to find her killer. Once she has seen all the passengers in the car, and is sure that he's not among them, she disappears to wait for the next car. One car allegedly knocked her off the road, only to see her again two miles further along the road, where she clung to the car until she had gazed at each person in the car.

The Starkweather Hitchhiker

Stories of women or teenage girls in white by the side of the road are common in legends throughout this country, and probably others as well. Sometimes, as in the stories above, they are looking for vengeance; others, like the famous case of Mary in Chicago, are hitchhiking. Mary simply wants a ride from town back to the cemetery where she is buried. Others just want to talk a bit, or perhaps to warm up, then leave the vehicle, like a young woman near Starkweather, in the northeast quarter of North Dakota.

An abandoned railroad track follows part of State Highway 20, the main road through Starkweather, and a spectral young woman is often seen by drivers passing through between dusk and dawn. At first glance she appears quite solid and real, but at second glance, she's gone. A longhaul trucker who knows the road well was driving north towards Starkweather one icy winter afternoon. He saw the young woman, really just a girl, he thought, walking along the tracks. Concerned for her welfare in the subzero weather, he pulled his rig to the side of the road and unfastened his seat belt. As he began to step down and out of his truck, he glanced at the passenger side. To his surprise and horror, the girl was sitting there, as white as the snow blanketing the prairie. He jumped back and out of his truck, and looked at the tracks and found them empty.

Swallowing hard, he started back into his truck. The cab was empty, but cold as ice, although the heater was blasting warm air. He felt the seat where the girl had been, and it too felt freezing to his touch.

The trucker says she was a pretty girl, about 17 or 18, and her clothing wasn't old fashioned. He, like many other people who've seen her, would like to know the whole story. Who was this girl? What happened to her? And why does she still haunt the highway near Starkweather?

Valley City's Old Broken Road

Valley City is a medium-sized town on Interstate 94, between Fargo to the east and Jamestown to the west. Like many towns its size, it has a college, and some businesses that continue to thrive against the odds. It also has more than its share of hauntings.

One of these hauntings occurs on an abandoned stretch of road only in use by area teenagers, who call it Old Broken Road because that's what it is. The sight they see is a large black dog with glowing red eyes, standing in the middle of the road. As you approach it in your car, they say, it just stands there, seeming to grow larger the closer you get. Just when you think you're going to hit it, it vanishes into the night.

So the legend of the black dog appears again in North Dakota. Is this dog a devil dog, warning Valley City's young people about the dangers of driving on a bad road in the darkness? Or is it just a story made up by one young person and believed so strongly by those who hear it that they see it too? No one knows for sure, but more than one Valley City teen told me that they had seen the spectral dog, and had never returned to Old Broken Road.

Old US Highway 2

US Highway 2 in northwest North Dakota, from Minot west to just past Stanley, was rerouted several years ago so that traffic could go around the towns along the old highway and travel more rapidly. But the old highway remains, and is in fairly good condition. At least, on the surface of the road it is.

But the towns it passes through – Des Lacs, Berthold, Tagus, Blaisdell, Palermo, and White Earth – are practically abandoned. Two of them, Tagus and Palermo, are officially "ghost towns" with fewer than ten inhabitants. This road is rarely traveled except by farmers who live in the area. And they only drive the old highway far enough to get to the new four-lane highway. But if you drive the highway at night, you'll see lights where there shouldn't be lights, in abandoned homes and collapsing barns, and you may see spectral old cars traveling towards you which vanish before you get close. Each small town has its own cemetery right along the road, and travelers who choose the old road over the new one report seeing shadowy figures bending over graves; some seem to be mourning, while others seem intent on more sinister purposes.

If you're traveling in that part of North Dakota, you may want to consider that the state Department of Transportation made the new highway for a purpose. Leave Old US 2 to the people who haunt it.

River Road in Bismarck

River Road, as you may guess from its name, runs along the Missouri River on the western edge of Bismarck. It's a city street, but people often drive it as if it were a highway. That has led to more than one accident, but perhaps the most tragic was the death of a young boy. He ran out into the road after a ball, and a car coming around the curve hit him, and he died.

Since his death, residents on River Road as well as those just driving it often see a young boy who appears as a light blue shadow, standing still in the middle of the street holding his ball. If the driver brakes, the boy disappears. If the driver keeps going, the car will go right through this spirit, and a chill will enter the car as it does. A reminder, perhaps, to keep the speed down?

Rural Road Legends

Like most places, North Dakota has plenty of what would be called urban legends in a more populated state. Here, we call them rural legends. These are stories with only one source, and no one to confirm or disprove them, but whose authenticity as history can only be considered dubious!

Sykeston
Just outside Sykeston (about fifteen miles west of Carrington in east central North Dakota) is a rest area, which is haunted by little girls. When women go into the ladies rooms, they can hear the children giggling and

whispering, yet when those women come out – no one is there! This is clearly not a malevolent haunting.

Kindred

A few miles north of Kindred, almost on the Minnesota border and south of North Dakota's center line, and heading towards Horace, just twenty or so short miles away, is an abandoned farmstead. People driving by at night will see a strange and unearthly light glowing from the barn's interior. When two travelers drove up the farm road to see the barn more closely, the car continued to drive toward this barn even after the driver put on the brakes! They were finally able to stop the car and speed away to the safety of their home.

Kathryn

In the small town of Kathryn, south of Valley City in east central North Dakota, there is a railroad bridge haunted by the ghost of a small girl. No one has been able to learn if a child died or was murdered near there. The ghost just stands on the bridge and looks at the passing cars.

Pisek

Near Pisek in northeastern North Dakota, south of Park River and southwest of Grafton, is a stretch of road known locally as Lovers Lane. There are tall old trees lining this gravel road, making it seem almost tunnel-like, especially on moonless nights. The story goes that if you stop your car there late at night, a small ghost-boy will appear and knock on your car doors and windows. There is also a rumor about a couple who made a suicide pact and hanged themselves from the trees; that story says that if you stop to make out, you'll hear their shoes scraping against the top of your car. As for me, I plan to avoid that road!

Fredonia

The Grim Reaper has apparently found a home in Fredonia, North Dakota, south and west of Jamestown in southeastern North Dakota. One story says that the Reaper lies in wait for those whose time is up. When they drive near him, he shows himself to them, and within only a few days, the unfortunates who have seen him will die. Another version says he leaps out of hiding and onto cars, but that may be more energetic than the truth.

Yet another version of Fredonia's Grim Reaper tells of a wedding that was held in the Berlin Baptist Church, west of Fredonia, and the reception for the wedding was held in Fredonia itself. One man, who had perhaps made too many toasts to the bride and groom, left the wedding in his car, heading for his home in Ashley, southwest of Fredonia and practically on the South Dakota border. The road he took followed the shore of a reservoir, twisting and turning along the former riverbed. At the last turn, he rolled his car, and died. His lights were seen by people on the other side of the lake, but they assumed he had just decided to stop for a while. His body was found the next day. Now he walks along the lake road wearing a white robe, but he isn't seen often.

Pingree

North of the town of Pingree, about fifteen miles north-northwest of Jamestown, lived a family named Moonie. Or perhaps it was a colony of Moonies, although that seems unlikely in rural North Dakota. Apparently these Moonies were inbred and more than slightly demented. They were in the habit of hiding in road ditches and throwing dead cats onto the road when cars came along, in the hopes that the cars would stop and they would scare the drivers. Since no driver from North Dakota would stop for a dead cat on the road, their little scheme didn't work very well, and apparently they gave it up. There are, it's said, ghosts of dead cats on the road north of Pingree to this day, only seen at night. No one knows what happened to the Moonies.

Fargo RR Tracks

While railroad tracks aren't quite the same as roads, they serve much the same purpose. A railroad track that runs through Fargo, on the eastern border of North Dakota, to Moorhead, on the western border of Minnesota, is haunted by the red-eyed ghost of a woman. This woman was trying to jump onto the train to get to Minnesota, but her grip missed and instead of riding, she was dragged through Fargo. Parts of her body were spread for several miles. (Interestingly, there is no official record of any woman dying on those tracks...) Her ghost is mostly seen by the homeless who camp along the tracks. She stares at them with her fierce red eyes, and since she won't disappear, they find new campsites.

Rugby

In northern North Dakota, U.S. Highway 2 is the main thoroughfare. Almost in the center of it is Rugby, which also happens to be the geographical center of North America. Outside of Rugby, cars speeding home see flashing Highway Patrol lights behind them. When they pull over and stop, the lights vanish. If you speed up again, the lights will reappear. Is this just a game that a patrolman is playing to make you slow down? Or is a ghostly Highway Patrol Officer still doing his job on Highway 2?

Mysterious Murders

On travel magazine lists of safe places to visit, and safest places to live surveys, North Dakota usually comes in first, and if not first, then in the top four safe places. Of course this hasn't always been true, but most North Dakotans would probably say that since 1900, this state has been safer than any other. And if someone is murdered here, the killer is almost always someone in the family – an angry drunk husband, a too-young mother of a colicky baby, or the thankfully rare family annihilator, like Gerald Grinde, who shot his wife and three children before killing himself in Grand Forks back in the mid-1980s. Killings by strangers are very rare; the authorities almost never have to look outside the family. But every once in a while, a murder comes along that has everyone shaking their heads and wondering how – or why – this could possibly have happened, and in some cases, continuing to wonder who really did it.

The Minister and the Maid
Krem (near Pick City)

In August of 1938, Lutheran minister Heio Janssen, a man not just respected but loved by the parishes he'd served since 1907, was convicted of murdering his 16-year-old maid, Alma Kruckenberg, and setting fire to the parsonage to hide his crime. People in the small town of Krem in Mercer County where Janssen's church was located couldn't believe that their pastor was capable of doing anything like that. When he was arrested, they flocked to the sheriff's office, and railed against the sheriff for having arrested him, because Heio Janssen could not possibly be guilty. Until he confessed. Then it became a why-dunnit, rather than a who-dunnit.

But where does this story really start? Did it start when 17-year-old Heio from a small town called Timmel in Germany took a ship, with his cousin Gehde, to Baltimore, then a train to Waverly, Iowa, where they enrolled in seminary school? We know very little about Heio Janssen's life before that voyage, and after that, all we really know is that he was a good student, at the top of his class, that he graduated in 1907, and was ordained on June 23rd of that year at a synod meeting in Mendota, Illinois, along with other candidates from other seminaries.

Around the time of his ordination, he married then-17-year-old Gertraude (Gertrude) Masuhr, like him a German immigrant, who had been living in an orphanage with her older sister, Margarete, since their mother died around 1892. With his wife and her sister, he moved west to North Dakota, to the community of Lincoln Valley in Sheridan County, where he served four surrounding congregations. In 1911, both he and Margarete patented land in Schiller township in Sheridan County, outside of the community of Lincoln Valley. He stayed there until 1915, when a land plat shows that he then owned the land patented by Margarete, and Margarete wasn't shown at all. He, his wife, and their two boys are listed in Sheridan County in the North Dakota state census of 1915, but Margarete is not, although she had been their closest neighbor in the 1910 federal census.

The Janssen family, without sister-in-law Margarete, moved to Miles City shortly after the 1915 survey, and Heio took over four area congregations from the previous minister. He left Miles City relatively soon, possibly because of a rearrangement of congregations and small churches, and arrived in Marsh, Montana, in 1920, shortly after their former pastor retired, just in time for the completion and dedication of Jehovah Lutheran Church in that community. He is remembered by one member of that congregation as a large and healthy Scandinavian man who spoke fluent German; it may be that his last name confused the congregation somewhat, as they were mainly Germans from Russia, but Heio Janssen was German through and through, although he became a nationalized American.

The congregation said that he was kind and pleasant to all he met, and lived his life devoted to God. He made regular visits to his many parishioners and seemed to enjoy their company. He was blessed with a loving wife and two healthy sons. Even then, however, his wife Gertrude was not well. She needed help around the house and with the boys, Erwin and Martin, just as she had in Miles City and Lincoln Valley. He stayed in Marsh for 13 years, until in 1933 he was transferred to Krem, North Dakota. Some in Marsh felt that he departed abruptly, but he said later that some of his parishioners didn't appreciate his efforts.

He was installed in the parish of Krem on October 29th, 1933. The parsonage, a lovely white two-story home, was next to the traditional white prairie church of the early 20th century: a white-painted wooden church with a high steeple. In early 1938, he hired 15-year-old Alma Kruckenberg, the 10th child and youngest daughter of Mr. and Mrs. John Kruckenberg, to help his wife around the house, to cook and to clean. His sons had long since moved out and on; Erwin had his own congregation in Montana, and Martin was finishing medical school in Illinois.

As seemed to be the pattern, Janssen was loved by his parishioners, who were regular in their attendance and enjoyed his sermons. But one August night in 1938, everything changed.

It had been a long hot summer, and the great drought of the 1930s continued in the area around Krem. The heat had made Gertrude's health worse, and on the morning of Monday, August 15th, 1938, Janssen drove Gertrude to nearby Stanton, where she caught the train that would take her to Bismarck for a scheduled medical procedure. He then returned to the parsonage in Krem.

The only account of what happened next came from Reverend Janssen himself, and he eventually told several different stories. What we do know is that very early Tuesday morning, neighbors woke to the scent of burning on the wind. About one a.m. he called his neighbors for help in putting out a fire in the parsonage, but by the time help arrived, the house was burning too fiercely for them to do anything except make sure it didn't spread to the neighboring church or start a grass fire. The house burned down completely, and Alma's bed on the second floor ended up in the basement, where neighbors, entering the home and looking for survivors, found it.

Alma's remains were still on her metal bed frame. Her head and limbs had been mostly burned away, leaving stumps to indicate where they had been, and her chest and abdominal walls had been burned away. Janssen appeared both distraught and horrified by the young girl's death. He said that he hadn't known she was there; that he thought she'd gone home since, with Gertrude gone, there would be little for her to do. He had awakened to find the entire house in flames, he said, then called for help. When asked how the fire had started, he said it must have been sparks from some papers he had burned in the basement furnace, since it was too hot to have fires in the home. When Coroner H.O. Chilson arrived from Beulah, he believed Janssen's grief and his story.

It wasn't until he examined Alma's body Tuesday afternoon that he saw something that made him call physicians F.R. Rasmussen and L.E. Rasmussen, both from Beulah. They examined the remains and confirmed his suspicion: Alma Kruckenberg, now just 16, was pregnant. At the same time, those examining the smoldering ruins of the parsonage found no evidence that anything had been burned in the furnace.

They felt they had no choice but to call in Mercer County State's Attorney Floyd Sperry, and they told him what had happened and what they'd discovered. Sperry decided he needed to question Janssen. As the questioning started, Janssen expressed surprise at Alma's condition; she had no boyfriends, how could she be pregnant? He denied having any physical relationship with the girl with whose safety he had been entrusted. Questioning continued, and Janssen continued to assert his innocence. In his frustration, Sperry called the State Attorney General's office in Bismarck, and James Austin drove up to join him. Even with the two of them, he continued to deny any guilt.

It was at this point that a group of citizens, who heard the spreading rumors of Janssen's involvement in the fire and with Alma, became outraged that authorities would believe such acts of their minister, and asked them to free him.

Frustrated, the two prosecutors told him that the girl had been expecting his baby, and showed him the fetus they had removed from Alma's body. He remained unmoved. They brought Alma's parents to see him. John Kruckenberg asked Heio Janssen, as his friend, if he had anything to do with Alma's death. Heio said firmly that he was innocent.

Finally, after hours of questioning, Chilson apparently suggested to the attorneys that they move the questioning to the room where Alma's remains were laid out, the fetus next to her. Standing beside the ruins of what had been a vital young girl, Heio Janssen broke down. He confessed that he had had relations with her, that she'd threatened to tell his wife, and he was desperate. He said first that he had given her some strychnine in a glass of wine and sent her to bed, then went down to his study and waited until he was sure she was dead, then set fire to his home. When asked how he could have done such a thing, he answered that he didn't know. He was quoted in the *Bismarck Tribune* as saying, "The devil overcame me. I did wrong."

After the confession, the attorneys rushed him to Mandan's midnight court, presided over by Judge H.L. Berry, because they felt that local people, after hearing his confession, might harm Rev. Janssen. In a version different from his first confession, he said he'd given strychnine to Alma when he returned from Stanton Monday morning, then sent her to bed while he worked on a sermon in the study. She became ill, with terrible, painful stomach cramps. Finally, he gave her more poison in a glass of wine, which she drank, and after cramping so severe that it caused her to fall from her bed, she died. Janssen said that at that point, he'd put her in her bed, removed his clothes except for his shoes and put on his nightshirt, and then set the house on fire.

The Kruckenbergs came to the trial as well. After hearing Janssen confess to what was at the very least the statutory rape of their daughter, followed by her murder, Mr. Kruckenberg told Janssen, "I forgive you." To reporters outside, Kruckenberg said, "We were the best friends he had... he was well respected, not only in this community but among ministers over the state."

In Judge Berry's court, Heio Janssen, for once soft-spoken instead of his typical thundering from his pulpit, admitted that he was the father of Alma's unborn child, that he had poisoned her, and that he had set fire to the house. He then said that he had tried to stop Alma from taking poison, something he hadn't said before. Berry was irate at the many conflicting stories that Janssen had told, and threatened to add perjury to the list of charges before him. When finally asked what his plea was, Janssen answered that he was guilty, and ready for his punishment. Judge Berry sentenced him to life in prison at the North Dakota State Penitentiary across the river from Mandan. He was taken there immediately.

Alma's funeral was held in German at her parents' farm, and at St. Paul's Evangelical Church, some fifteen miles from the Krem Church, in English and German. She was buried in her family's cemetery; her pallbearers were six boys from her class in school.

Gertrude Janssen, still in the hospital in Bismarck, wasn't told of the events until Friday, when her husband was already in prison. When she was able to travel, she went to the home of her son Erwin Janssen in Montana.

The story was so sordid that it spread to papers across the country, as far away as St. Petersburg, Florida. It also appeared in the paper in Marsh, Montana, where people began to remember the drowning of teen-aged Rosa Opp in 1930. Rosa worked for Charles Krug, an area rancher with an enormous ranch. Her father, Daniel Opp, worked for the railroad but also had a small ranch, and he served as a deacon while Reverend Janssen served in Marsh. Rosa was a pretty, lively girl, friendly to everyone. Just before she disappeared in mid-August, 1930, she was excited about acting as a Confirmation Sponsor for her nephew Alvin, the son of her sister Lydia and her husband, which was to have occurred just a few days after the day she disappeared. Rosa's body was found September 15th, washed up against a tree on an island in the Yellowstone River. The coroner determined her death to have been suicide, but her family and friends would never believe it. Some fifty years later, her sister Emma wrote, "only God knows what really happened to her."

She was buried in Marsh, and Heio Janssen conducted her funeral service. Eight years later, reading the story of Alma Kruckenberg, the people of Marsh wondered if their own minister could have been involved in Rosa's death. He had, after all, told children to stay away from the artesian well that was just across the road from the church. She could have been drowned there, then been thrown into the river. However, there was, and is, simply no evidence connecting Rosa to Reverend Janssen.

That didn't stop authorities, and apparently reporters, from questioning Janssen about Rosa's death. It was also rumored that his sister-in-law, Margarete, had "disappeared" and was probably dead as well. One paper reported that he admitted to having "intimate relations" with Margarete, but denied having anything to do with her disappearance or with Rosa's death.

In 1957, a pulp magazine called *True Police Yearbook* resurrected the story, and retold it luridly, embellished with more fiction than fact. They wrote that W. J. Austin, a special state's attorney who had truly been appointed to handle the Janssen trial, questioned him regarding the disappearance of his wife's "voluptuous" sister from Lincoln Valley, implying that the disappearance had caused his congregation to push him out of town, and that another, equally lovely, sister had also mysteriously disappeared. And then there was the mysterious drowning of "15 year old" (the pulp writer's error) Rosa Opp, another beautiful girl to whom Janssen, they wrote, was "paternally attentive."

Actually, Margarete didn't disappear. She married a man named George Beaumont who was working on the railroad, and they settled first in Montana, and then in Pine Bluff, Arkansas, where she died in November of 1971 at the age of 84.

Gertrude apparently stopped communication with Margarete after her marriage to George. Why the sisters had a "falling out" we'll never know, as Margarete had no children, and Gertrude never discussed it with her sons, nor did she tell them that she had a younger sister, Alma, who was adopted as an infant by a family named Flitch, and went with them to Wisconsin, where as an adult, she married a man named Peter Udelhoven.

One question still remains: Why would Heio Janssen, a man of 51, an ordained minister who had been drawn to serve God at the age of 17, and preached in so many places, to parishioners who loved and respected him, do such a thing? Lust may have led him to Alma Kruckenberg's bed, as Gertrude may have been too ill to perform her "wifely duties," but to poison and murder two people, since Alma's unborn child died with her, seems almost unbelievable. Certainly his Krem congregation didn't believe it, not until they heard his confession. Perhaps it really was the devil, taking over his body and soul for a while. That was the only reason Heio Janssen could give for his hideous crime.

Heio Janssen died in prison in 1946, after an 8-month illness spent in the prison infirmary. He was buried without ceremony in the Potter's Field portion of Bismarck's Fairview Cemetery. He apparently rests quietly, but there are stories that a young woman in white haunts the grassy field where the Krem parsonage once stood. Does Alma still suffer, and fear her tormentor? I hope not. She suffered enough in her short life.

A Family Annihilated
Turtle Lake

A quiet farmhouse just three miles north of the pretty little town of Turtle Lake was the scene of what is probably the most brutal and heinous crime in North Dakota's history. Eight people were slaughtered with a shotgun and an axe, leaving only an eight-month-old baby alive. The farmhouse has long since fallen down, but memories of that grisly day haunt the area and those residents who can still remember what happened.

Thursday, April 22, 1920, was a pleasant spring day, just warm enough for Beata Wolf to start the laundry after breakfast, and start hanging it on the line. Her husband, Jacob Wolf, a quiet and friendly man, was caring for the livestock in the barn and hog pen, while two of their six daughters were gathering eggs in the chicken house. Someone arrived at their home, and chaos and tragedy followed in his wake.

Just two days later, on the morning of Saturday, April 24, a neighbor named John Kraft was passing by the Wolf home. North Dakota's ever-changing weather made Saturday a cold, drizzling day, and John immediately noticed the laundry hanging on Mrs. Wolf's clothes line. Knowing what a good housewife Beata was, and that she'd never leave her laundry in the rain, he sensed that something must be wrong, and he pulled up to the house.

He called out, but heard no answer but the grunting of pigs coming from the barn. He ran into the barn, to find the body of his friend Jacob Wolf, partly covered with straw, and with hogs eating from the side of his body. He looked around in horror, and saw that two of the girls also lay nearby, their bodies partially covered with straw. He drove the pigs back into their pens, then rushed to Turtle Lake for help.

Wolf Family Memorial ("Die Ermordete Familie").

Kraft returned with McLean County Sheriff O.E. Stefferud and a doctor, and they were followed by a reporter from the *Turtle Lake Wave*, a weekly newspaper that came out Fridays. They were also followed by many curious people from town, which would later make the investigation more difficult. Back at the farm, the sheriff looked at the bodies of Jacob Wolf and the two girls in the barn, then, along with Kraft, searched the other buildings. In the house, they found a blood-stained axe on the kitchen floor, and while an attempt had been made to clean the floor, a bloody trail left by bodies dragged to the stairway to the cellar led them to their next discovery.

In the cellar were the bodies of Mrs. Wolf, three of her daughters, and 13-year-old Jacob Hofer, the Wolf family's hired boy. A weak crying led the men to the main bedroom, where they found baby Emma Wolf, just 8 months old, alive in her cradle. Although she was dehydrated and thirsty, she was otherwise unharmed – and the sole survivor of her family.

The local paper and the daily *Bismarck Tribune*, which jumped on the story and printed it in the Saturday evening edition, April 24th, described in detail how each family member had been killed. Mr. Wolf, aged 41, had been shot once from long range, then received a short-range shotgun blast to his side that tore three ribs from his side and probably resulted in his instant death. He was believed to have died in the barn. Mrs. Wolf, 35 at the time of her death, was shot once in the back at close range, but had no other wounds. Her body was dragged from the kitchen to the cellar. The eldest daughter, Bertha, was shot in the face, also at close range, and then, the doctor believed, was struck in her already damaged head with the axe, her head nearly severed from her body. Daughter Maria, 10 years old, was shot in the back of the head; the shotgun was close enough that her hair and neck received powder burns. Edna, just 8, was also shot in the back of the head, a blast that tore part of the top of her head off. Six-year-old Lydia was shot behind her left ear, then took an axe blow to the base of her head. Little Martha, just three years old, was the only one not shot with the shotgun. She was struck in the forehead with the back of the axe, pushing her skull into her brain. Jacob Hofer was shot through the neck from behind, a blow that severed his trachea along with a carotid artery.

Only two shotgun shells were found on the scene, both in the hayloft; no shotgun was found. It was believed that Mr. Wolf's shotgun was used in the murders. No motive could be discovered for the killings; Mr. Wolf had cash and some "valuable papers," possibly stock certificates, in a small portable safe in the bedroom, but the safe was untouched, and nothing was missing from the house, which removed robbery as a motive. No one who knew Mr. Wolf could believe he or his family had any enemies. A theory that Mr. Wolf killed his family and then himself was dismissed both because of the absence of the shotgun and shells, and the position of his wounds.

While the sheriff and his deputies searched for clues and questioned possible witnesses, an inquest into the deaths was held on Sunday. A doctor testified that all eight deaths were instantaneous. He further stated that since little Emma's window had been open from Thursday until she was found on Saturday, and she was wearing very little clothing and the weather had been cold and rainy, that someone must have returned to the Wolf home before the bodies were discovered and fed and changed her, or she wouldn't have survived. She had been taken in by an aunt and uncle when the Wolf family murder was discovered.

During the Sunday search, a neighbor alerted the sheriff to a broken shotgun in a slough near the Wolf home. The two-barreled shotgun was only very slightly rusted, indicating that it hadn't been in the slough long. Authorities believed this was the gun used to kill members of the Wolf family, and began to search for its owner. At this point, authorities believed that at least two people had been involved in the gruesome murders, although no motive could be determined.

State Attorney William Langer (later a North Dakota governor) went to Turtle Lake on Monday the 26th to take charge of the case, which by now was the center of attention of the entire state. Langer had urged the governor to offer an award for the conviction of the two men believed to have committed the crime, and he announced that he had hired agents from "a national famous detective agency" and that the men would arrive in Turtle Lake within the next two days. Bloodhounds from the State Penitentiary had already been working, but between the number of people who had visited the crime scene and the amount of rain that had fallen between Thursday and Saturday afternoon, they had no real success.

On Wednesday the 28th, with authorities no closer to finding a solution to the crime, a funeral was held for the Wolf family and Jacob Hofer. Turtle Lake was nearly overrun with visitors who had come to pay their respects and attend the funeral; some had come from as far as 300 miles away. After a funeral service conducted in German by Reverend Rummel of the Baptist Church, over 450 cars joined the funeral procession to the cemetery. The family and Jacob were buried in a single grave, now marked with an enormous black marble cross that reads, "Die Ermordete Familie," or "The Murdered Family." A hedge of lilacs, Beata Wolf's favorite flowers, covers the grave, and on the far side there are small black marble markers for each victim, with their names, date of birth, and date of death.

The story of the murders and the search for the killers continued to fill the front pages of newspapers across the state. On Thursday, April 29th, the Bismarck Tribune's front page announced that arrests could be made as soon as that day. An unnamed man who was described as the closest neighbor to the Wolf farm had already been questioned several times. This man, authorities believed, was the only man in the region with whom Wolf had any differences. Some of the friction was related to free range cattle; it was said that the man accused Wolf of taking some of his cattle and claiming them as his own.

This suspect also had been spreading a story about a relationship between Wolf and another farmer's daughter, a rumor that was blatantly false. The suspect's 9-year-old daughter, Blanche, whom the newspaper described as being "about 12 years of age," told questioning authorities that her father had been away from home most of one day the previous week, but she couldn't remember which day. She was questioned while her parents attended the Wolf funeral.

Wolf Family Members, Remembered.
Turtle Lake, North Dakota.

Besides this neighbor, authorities were still searching for two men in a car who had threatened a farmer's son with a shotgun on the day of the murders, ordering him to bring them gasoline from his father's tank. They had been sought since that Thursday, but hadn't been found. Rumors of actual arrests made in other papers were denied by authorities in the Tribune's copy.

Friday's headlines announced a reward of $1,000 to anyone who could bring the murderer or murderers to justice. The money was raised by McLean County officials and Attorney General William Langer; Governor Frazier still refused to use any state funds in a reward. No arrests were imminent, or if they were, they weren't announced.

Finally, on Thursday, May 13th, the front page headline "Farmer Confesses Turtle Lake Murder" was just under the top headline, "Langer Wins For Governor" in the *Bismarck Tribune*. Farmer Henry Layer, a neighbor to the Wolf family who was married and had six children of his own, the youngest a baby boy about the same age as Emma Wolf, had been arrested quietly on May 11th, and questioned for forty-eight hours until he broke, and gave authorities the confession they wanted.

His confession appeared in papers all over the state, but was probably given the most notice in the *Bismarck Tribune* and the *Turtle Lake Wave*. He told authorities that he'd visited the Wolf farm to ask Jacob Wolf for money for one of his cows that had been severely injured by the Wolf family's dog. Wolf had seized and loaded his own shotgun, Layer continued, and the two men had struggled over the gun. During the struggle the gun went off, killing Mrs. Wolf.

Layer went on to say that he had shot Mr. Wolf, and then the rest of the family, along with Jacob Hofer, getting ammunition from the bureau drawer inside the house. He made no mention of using the axe, nor did he give a reason for killing the rest of the family after accidentally killing Mrs. Wolf. When asked why he hadn't killed Emma, he replied, "because I did not go into the room where the baby lay." He admitted breaking the shotgun and dumping it in the slough, and said that he had washed his hands there. Then, he said, he had returned home and continued plowing his fields.

Apparently authorities, in the persons of Bismarck Police Chief Chris Martinson and McLean County Sheriff Ole Stefferud, had been watching him since Saturday, April 24th, when he accompanied searchers at the Wolf farm and found two shotgun shells in the hayloft, which, in his confession, he said he had tossed there before leaving. On Sunday morning, he returned to gaze at the bodies of Wolf and the two daughters, still in the barn, and his face was completely blank, which unsettled Martinson.

Layer, his wife, and their only daughter, 9-year-old Blanche, attended the Wolf family funeral, and although the *Bismarck Tribune*'s report of the funeral immediately after it was held said only, "...the lids were lifted from each of the coffins..." the sheriff said that Layer had insisted that the lids be opened so he could look into each face.

After he signed the confession, which was probably written out for him, Layer went to sleep, an action that police and the sheriff took to signify that he was a soulless killer. After forty-eight hours of questioning which probably included the use of clubs, fists, and boots, the man may have been simply exhausted. He was then taken before Washburn judge W.L. Nuessle, convicted of murder, and sentenced to life with hard labor in the State Penitentiary of Bismarck, where he was taken immediately. A year later he appealed, asking for a new trial on the grounds that his confession was false and had been coerced, but the appeal was denied.

In March of 1925, Henry Layer had surgery to remove his appendix, which had been giving him bouts of appendicitis throughout the time he'd been in prison. The surgery didn't go well, and a blood clot went into his heart. About three hours before he died, he told Warden Lee that he was innocent. He had spoken with his aging mother and a brother the previous night, and had told them both that he was innocent. A prison guard, who remained nameless, told the Washburn Leader reporter that he'd overheard Layer say, "I did not do it alone." Yet another nameless guard said he'd heard Layer say, "My eyes are guilty, but my hands are free of their blood" in reference to the Wolf family. Layer had told the warden about a year before his death that the murders had been committed by a man who was subsequently committed to the State Hospital for the Insane, as it was called at the time, but refused to give the inmate's name, saying that he had died in the asylum. No one believed him.

Like Heio Janssen, Henry Layer is buried in Potter's Field in an unmarked grave, in Fairview Cemetery in northeast Bismarck. Two families were destroyed by this crime. The Wolf family perished, except for Emma, whose aunt and uncle raised her as their own. She visited her family's grave in the Turtle Lake cemetery each Memorial Day until her own death in 2002.

Henry Layer's wife, Lydia, couldn't maintain the farm on her own; she had to separate her six children. Four of the children, oldest daughter Blanche and sons Berthold, Edwin, Alvin, and Emil, were sent to the Ward Home in Fairmont, Minnesota. Tragically, Berthold was killed at the age of 6 when a wagon filled with sugar beets backed over his head. The other three may have stayed with Lydia and a grandmother, although whether that person was Lydia's mother or Henry's is unclear. Lydia found a job in Bismarck, but her life was not a happy one.

The only ones who profited from the conviction of Henry Layer were Police Chief Martinson of Bismarck, who was given the $1,000 reward for his work in obtaining a confession; Sheriff Ole Stafferud, who was given an award by a police organization; and William Langer, whose work and prominence in the Wolf case undoubtedly helped him win the Republican candidacy for the up-coming gubernatorial election.

Many people still question Layer's conviction. The strongest theory is that his confession was coerced, by brutality, at the suggestion – or order – of State Attorney General Langer, who badly needed this case to be closed. Another theory is that if Layer was guilty, he didn't commit the crimes alone. From the first, authorities believed they were looking for at least two men, and those who believe this point to the fact that Layer never mentioned the use of the axe, as well as the fact that he was not likely to have known where the ammunition for Wolf's shotgun was, given that the two were not friendly. It was also reported that two boys from the family that bought the Wolf farm after the family died found two black masks in some brush near the back door. But as far as McLean County is concerned, the case is closed, the killer confessed, and all involved are now deceased.

Still, it's been said that for many years Beata Wolf haunted the Wolf farm, looking for her daughters, and calling out for Emma. Now, there are rumors that Emma's spirit haunts the cemetery, staying near her family's grave site and weeping, just as she did in life. This story brought only sadness to most of those involved, and despite the status of the "case," the real murderers are still a mystery to many who know of this horrific slaughter of innocents.

The Missing Olsons
Hettinger

Yvonne and Norman Olson had lived in Hettinger, a small town in southwestern North Dakota, all their lives. They had raised three children there, and almost everyone in town knew them. Yvonne was a healthy and active 69-year-old, while Norman, at the age of 73, was struggling with depression and the early stages of Alzheimer's disease. Although Yvonne had told close friends that his moods had become less stable, and talking to him was like tiptoeing through a minefield, to avoid setting his temper off, she never expressed any fear of him to anyone.

Something happened on Saturday, August 14th, 2004. The couple apparently left their home in a hurry; there was a coffeepot still turned on, and when the house was searched a couple of days later, the searchers found spoiled food on the counter. They also found Yvonne's purse, with her keys, cash, and checkbook, in the home, and her glasses, which she absolutely needed in order to see, on the garage floor. Norman's medications for depression and Alzheimer's were also still in the home. The couple's 1999 tan Ford Taurus was missing. Despite these findings, the North Dakota State Bureau of Investigation (BCI) didn't find any signs of a struggle.

Neighbors contacted their daughter, Jackie Muggerud, after not seeing the Olsons for a couple of days, and she reported her parents missing to the Adams County Sheriff. She returned to her Hettinger home from a visit to her children, and her two brothers living in Arizona also flew in to join her. An official search began on August 16th, with authorities performing a ground search within a fifteen-mile radius of the home to try to find the couple or their car, focusing on abandoned farmsteads and shelterbelts where the vehicle could have been hidden from view. By Thursday, August 19th, the search range increased, and National Guard helicopters flew over southwestern North Dakota, looking for a parked vehicle. The Civil Air Patrol joined the search on Friday and Saturday. The Sheriff announced on the 21st that he believed a .22-caliber revolver might be missing from the home.

The search continued for days, then weeks, as people from the county, then from all around the state, joined in. Hunters familiar with the area arrived to help, as did people on horseback, and others searched on foot.

On August 24th, the Olson children went on television to ask for help in finding their parents. The last time anyone had seen the Olsons was August 13th, when Yvonne was in the grocery store. She'd been organizing a bake sale to raise funds for her niece's upcoming kidney transplant, and her freezer was stuffed with baked goods. The children went to their parents' home each night, leaving everything untouched, to try to come up with ideas. They contacted a national missing persons group called missingadults.org, and they put up missing posters all over Adams county and sent them to counties around the state to be put up. As the search continued, the Olson children first hired a private investigator, and then a nationally known psychic who had worked with police in several hundred cases.

On November 4th, nearly three months after the Olsons vanished, their car was finally found by a pheasant hunter, inside a Quonset building rented by the hunter, about eight miles from Hettinger. The Adams County Sheriff acknowledged that searchers had looked in that area, but said that he didn't think anyone had looked inside the building. The car held no evidence of the Olsons except a denim jacket that Jackie Muggerud thought might be her father's. The car looked like it had been parked in the building, then had the doors closed behind it, and whoever had left it had walked – or driven – away.

The hunter who found the car is also a police officer from Fargo. He'd parked near the Quonset building and gone hunting for half an hour or so, then returned to his truck. It was then he noticed that there was a 3 to 4 inch gap in the building's sliding door. He looked through the gap, and saw a car with a Ford logo on it. He went to the nearby home of a hunter friend and told him about the car, and the friend knew that the missing Olson car was a Ford. They went back to the building together, opened the door, and walked around the car, careful not to disturb anything. Then they called the sheriff's department.

The local farmer who owned the Quonset said he hadn't been to the building since the spring, when he'd moved out some haying equipment he'd stored there. The farmer had joined the search for the Olsons, and looked all around his property, but hadn't thought to look inside the Quonset. He said to reach it, you'd have to travel about a mile on a two-track (unpaved and not graveled) section line track, so unless you knew it was there, you weren't likely to find it. He said he'd thought the sheriff's department or another searcher would have looked inside the building. The farmer had known Norman Olson all his life, and said that he'd never seen either of the Olsons in the area of the building, nor could he think of a reason why they would ever be there.

Jackie Muggerud told reporters that seeing Sheriff Molbert at her door that night was "almost surreal." She said she was trying to stay positive. In the meantime, while a deputy kept watch on the Quonset to see if anyone might return to it, the sheriff met with five BCI agents to decide their next step. They thought they'd conduct another horse-back search and possibly get a bloodhound from the Burleigh County Sheriff's department.

Two days after finding the car, searchers on foot discovered human remains in an abandoned and dilapidated farmhouse (November 6th). Although the Sheriff's Department felt that the remains might be those of Yvonne Olson, he declined to confirm it until the remains had been examined by the coroner and both the identity and cause of death were confirmed.

At this point, Jackie Muggerud was overwhelmed and needed time alone. Her two brothers decided to return to their homes in Phoenix, and to wait and see what further searching and examination of the remains could come up with.

On November 9th, authorities confirmed that the remains found on the 6th were those of Yvonne Olson, although the cause of death hadn't yet been determined. The medical examiner said that he hadn't yet ascertained how long she had been dead. A representative of the Olson family said that it appeared that someone had tried to hide her body, found in the basement of the house. It looked as if someone had put some of the wood debris from the house around the body to try and cover it.

The next day the Adams County Sheriff said that the preliminary autopsy reports indicated that Yvonne Olson had been killed by a gunshot wound. He didn't know what type of gun had been used, and he said that they had still not located the .22-caliber handgun believed missing from the Olsons' home. The North Dakota Governor authorized the National Guard to help in continuing search efforts to find Norman Olson, who was presumed dead.

Over the next two weeks, the search for Norman Olson continued, on foot, on 4-wheelers, on horseback, and from the air. Off-duty police officers and deputies from neighboring counties joined the search, as did farmers and ranchers from around Hettinger. The National Guard and cadaver dogs joined the search, too. The main search area was now a five-mile area around the Quonset building where Olson's car had been found. Some areas that had not previously been searched were included this time.

When Norman Olson's remains were finally found on November 24th, authorities should have shown some embarrassment. A South Dakota volunteer, Tami Bulik, with her cadaver dog, Lilly, went back to the area where Yvonne Olson's body had been found, and the dog led her to Olson's body, which was in the attic of the building whose basement had held the remains of Yvonne Olson. The body was stuffed headfirst into a 30-gallon drum, and a .22-caliber revolver "similar" to Olson's was found with the body.

Bulik wouldn't accept the praise for finding the remains. She said that all the credit went to Lilly, who had brought searchers to that site twice before, and continued to do the posture that indicated she had found remains, then tried to climb the north wall of the building. Bulik said she braced herself between two of the crumbling walls and could see into the attic, and saw the remains. The attic had no stairway; there were rotting ladder steps up one wall that were nearly impossible to climb.

Sheriff Molbert had mixed reactions. He was relieved that the remains had been found, but had trouble believing they'd been missed when Yvonne Olson's remains had been found and removed earlier in the month. Bulik said she understood why they were missed; they were nearly impossible to see from outside. If Lilly hadn't tried to climb up the house, she might have missed them again.

When the remains were carefully removed on the 26th, the sheriff described the attic area where they'd been found as "an enclosed ceiling." When they'd looked before, the attic appeared vacant except for a barrel – the other end of the barrel in which Olson's remains were found. The sheriff went on to say that the body was partially covered with garbage, wood debris and other materials.

The Olson children were upset that the remains of Norman Olson hadn't been found when Yvonne's were. Blake Olson stated that he felt that the searchers didn't do their job, and the family had been left to grieve and wonder for weeks.

When the BCI completed examination of all the evidence, including the remains, they closed the case, concluding that Norman Olson had forced his wife to accompany him in their car to the Quonset building, then forced her to go with him to the collapsing house. There, they say, he shot and killed her, and stuffed her body into the basement or crawl space beneath the farmhouse. He then managed to get into the attic and tried to crawl into the barrel, and killed himself with his own gun.

Rev. John Mathai, the Olsons' priest at Holy Trinity Catholic Church in Hettinger, found this unbelievable. He couldn't believe that Norman, even with early Alzheimer's, would have killed his wife of forty-nine years, then kill himself. He hoped that the BCI would continue the investigation. The Olson family, too, believed that Norman wouldn't – and probably couldn't – have killed his wife and then himself, especially with the complex plan of hiding the car in the Quonset and hiding both bodies in the ruined building. They had trouble imagining a motive for anyone to kill their parents, but they pointed out that Norman's wallet and wedding ring were never found.

When the sheriff had difficulty gaining access to the attic where Norman's body was found, he had to have wondered how an elderly man with Alzheimer's could have managed it. When Bulik's dog, Lilly, found Norman two weeks after finding Yvonne's body in the same building, she explained that dogs can't always pick up scents; wind conditions and moisture can affect their ability to find a body, especially if there are two in the same place. Another possibility never brought up by officials is that Norman's body may not have been there when Yvonne's was found. A third person could have brought a ladder, and used that to get Norman and the barrel into that "enclosed ceiling."

The police paid little attention to either the private investigator hired by the Olsons' children or the psychic they hired. If more attention had been paid, would the bodies have been found sooner? According to author William Jackson, Noreen Renier psychically saw Norman Olson struggling with an intruder who then forced Olson to drive the intruder and Yvonne to a spot that eerily resembled the place with the Quonset building where the Olson's car had been found. She described the intruder as a young Caucasian male with curly dark hair, someone who was a liar and had been in trouble in the past. She described his vehicle as a tan pickup truck with a North Dakota license plate, and gave some of the numbers on it. If the police had seriously searched for this vehicle, what might they have found?

The case is considered closed now, and we'll never know what authorities might have found if they'd listened to the psychic, and to the family, who believed that their father would not have been emotionally or physically able to kill their mother. But many in Hettinger, and in the rest of North Dakota too, still wonder who really killed Yvonne and Norman Olson.

Native American Spirits, Stories, and Sacred Places

North Dakota has four reservations within its boundaries. Northern-most is the Turtle Mountain Reservation, home to the Turtle Mountain Band of Chippewa (also called Ojibwe). In northeastern North Dakota, south of Devils Lake, is the Spirit Lake Reservation, home to the Sisseton Wahpeton Sioux band. In the northwestern quarter of the state is Fort Berthold Reservation; the three affiliated tribes, the Mandan, Hidatsa, and Arikara, share the reservation. The Standing Rock reservation is south and west of Bismarck, with the Missouri River as its eastern boundary in North Dakota, and it stretches over the state line into South Dakota. Most of the population in North Dakota are Upper and Lower Yanktonai Dakota, while the population in South Dakota includes Lakota from the Hunkpapa and Sihapsa bands.

The native peoples, or First Nations, play a major role in both North Dakota's history and its present day life. But they are largely misunderstood by most outsiders. As one of those outsiders, I am approaching their stories and culture with respect, and any errors I make are my own.

One major area of mistakes lie in the area of language. When trying to translate Dakota words into English, English speakers make the mistake of trying to fit the meanings into their own culture, rather than interpreting them in their culture of origin. This is evident in the Devils Lake/Spirit Lake name difference – neither of which exactly fits the original name of the area, Mne Wakan. "Mne" does mean water; that part is fairly straightforward. But "Wakan" is not the same as "spirit" and certainly not the same as "devil." The "devil" translation comes from early missionaries, who felt that anything sacred to non-Christians must come from the Devil.

Albert White Hat Sr., a Lakota elder from the Rosebud Reservation in South Dakota, is the author of *Writing and Reading the Lakota Language* and has been a teacher and scholar for most of his life. Speaking to students at the United Tribes Technical College in Bismarck, he said, "Language is a living being." He describes it as a "carrier of culture," something that will transport history, values, and culture from each generation to the one that follows. He points out that Christians of European descent translated the word "wakan" as "sacred, holy, mystery," but the true meaning is completely different. White Hat says that "kan" means life or energy, and "wa" is the being that carries the "kan." That means that all people, First Nation or not, and all living beings, are wakan.

White Hat further explains that many Lakota words are forced to fit Christian concepts. He says that Lakota do not have a religion, as Christians and others do; what they have is spirituality, which is practiced in the four vital virtues of the Lakota culture: bravery, generosity, fortitude, and wisdom. Much the same could probably be said of other First Nation peoples in the state, although many on the Turtle Mountain Reservation practice Catholicism.

Spirits, to First Nation peoples, aren't necessarily the ghosts of dead people, although they can be. Not all ghosts are evil, though; they may be humorous, or just sad. Trees, rocks, the sun and moon, plants and animals – all have spirits, and should be respected. There are many places that are sacred, although sometimes they are sacred to those who no longer live in the area. Some stories tell of monsters, and some of heroes. Storytelling is still a valued skill among the First Nations, and the favorite stories almost always involve a spirit, a hero, or a mystery.

Sitting Bull's Grave
Standing Rock Reservation

History books in American schools describe Sitting Bull, if they mention him at all, as one of the leaders who defeated Custer and the Seventh Cavalry at the Battle of the Little Big Horn. But to the Lakota, Sitting Bull, or *Tatanka Iyotake*, a member of the Hunkpapa band, was a great leader whose life exemplified the virtues of fortitude, bravery, generosity, and wisdom. His purpose was always to protect his people and to care for them. As a boy, his name was "Slow," not because he was thought to be stupid or because he couldn't run quickly, but because he always stopped to consider before he acted, a characteristic that he retained throughout his life. He wasn't a hot-tempered man, nor did he consider himself a hero. He was a humble man, taking pride in his people rather than himself, and he never tried to put himself above others.

Sitting Bull was killed, and some say deliberately murdered, in a battle with U.S. soldiers and "Indian police" on July 15, 1890. The American authorities believed that Sitting Bull was involved in the Ghost Dance movement that culminated, for the Lakota, in the massacre at Wounded Knee, and knowing how powerful and respected Sitting Bull was, those authorities feared him. Whether they murdered him or not, they were undoubtedly relieved by his death.

After his death, Sitting Bull's remains were buried in a small grave near Fort Yates, on the North Dakota side of the reservation. The grave was not clearly marked, and after many years, became neglected. The grave site was privately owned, so the grave didn't belong to the Dakota people. Early in the 1950s, a white businessman from Mobridge, South Dakota, approached the owner of the grave site and asked for permission to move the remains of Sitting Bull to South Dakota, but he was refused.

This was the point, legend says, when a group of South Dakota Lakota along with a mortician came to North Dakota during a blizzard, and dug up Sitting Bull's remains. They took them down to South Dakota and reburied them. This site is marked with a six-foot tall granite bust of Sitting Bull atop an eight-foot pedestal, donated by sculptor Korczak Ziolkowski, designer of the Crazy Horse mountain monument still under construction in the Black Hills of South Dakota.

The site is on fee land: land inside the reservation boundaries, but privately owned. In 2005, two men, one a Dakota from the reservation, the other a white man who had been an environmental consultant, purchased the land for an estimated $55,000. At the time they purchased it, the site was covered in trash, and the pedestal pocked with bullet holes. Their intention was to turn the site into a memorial complex with an interpretive center, a gift shop, a snack bar and a restaurant. Ernie LaPointe, recognized as Sitting Bull's closest living relative by the Smithsonian Institution, is fighting this plan. He wants his great-grandfather to be re-buried at the Little Big Horn battle site, along with leggings and a lock of Sitting Bull's hair taken after his death and kept at the Smithsonian until they were returned to LaPointe in 2007.

The Lakota of North Dakota maintain that Sitting Bull's remains are still at the original burial site, owned and managed by the SHSND since 1956. In January of 2007, the ownership was transferred back to the Standing Rock Sioux tribe. Some say only part of the remains were taken, so some are still in North Dakota. Others say that another man was buried on top of Sitting Bull so that if anyone tried to steal the remains, they wouldn't get them, so all of Sitting Bull's remains are still at the original burial site.

One other story is told as well. After Sitting Bull's death, another man, chosen by Sitting Bull himself, was buried in the spot marked as Sitting Bull's grave, but his remains were taken by his Dakota mother's family up to Canada, where they rest in quiet dignity.

Without the possibility of DNA testing, which is unlikely given the Native American Graves Protection and Repatriation Act, which states that removal of remains, even on private land, require the consent of the tribe, the world may never be entirely certain where Sitting Bull is truly buried.

White Buffalo Calf Woman
A Sacred Story

According to traditions of the People (the Dakota and Lakota and also Nakota, called Assiniboine), a Spirit Woman named White Buffalo Calf Woman appeared to the People nineteen generations ago. She taught them seven healing rites, which have been passed down from generation to generation, and gave them a sacred pipe. She brought these things to help the People while they were undergoing a difficult time. She told them that they would also help with even more difficult times that would come in the future. In each generation, there is a keeper of the sacred pipe bundle.

The purpose of the pipe and the healing rites was in part to help the People hold on to their culture and their way of life, to help them stay connected to who they are. The *inikag'a*, often called a sweat lodge by outsiders, is used in all healing rites, at the beginning and the end of each rite, as is the sacred eagle feather, which represents the collected wisdom of the People.

White Buffalo Calf Woman prophesied that she would return to the earth at the worst time. According to the current keeper of the sacred pipe bundle, that time began in 1994, with the birth of a white buffalo. Now not only the buffalo, but many other animals are showing the sacred white color. White Buffalo Calf Woman said that when this happened terrible changes would happen. The climate would change, the earth would change, there would be new diseases never seen before, and there would be a shocking lack of respect among the humans on the earth for each other, and for life itself. If the People don't return to their traditional and sacred ways, the current keeper of the sacred bundle may be the last keeper.

Other traditions agree that the birth of the white buffalo signals a time of change, but they say that it will be the beginning of a good change, a return by all people to the values of traditional People: honoring the earth and each other, giving gifts to the plants and animals that nourish us, and respecting ourselves and others. For them, the birth of a sacred white buffalo is a reason to celebrate. The first one was named Miracle; he was born at the farm of Dave Heider in Wisconsin.

In the buffalo herd that roams the grounds of the National Buffalo Museum at Jamestown, North Dakota, an albino buffalo cow named White Cloud, born in 1996, can often be seen from the highway. She belongs to Daniel and Jean Shirek of Michigan, North Dakota, and is leased by the Museum. White Cloud has since given birth to a white bull buffalo calf in 2007. He was named Dakota Miracle. In 2008, another albino buffalo was born to White Cloud after she was bred to one of her brown bull sons who carries the albino gene. The odds of three white buffalo in one herd? Since no one can compute the odds of one white buffalo in a herd, it seems impossible to know the likelihood of three.

The white buffalo have brought people from all over the world, people who have heard the story of White Buffalo Calf Woman. They leave gifts for the buffalo, often tying flags to the fence to commemorate their visit. I don't know what they take with them. I do know that after seeing these amazing, special, and yes, sacred animals, I left with a sense of wonder and of hope.

On-A-Slant Village

Mandan

On the grounds of Fort Abraham Lincoln State Park, about four miles south of Mandan, is a partial reconstruction of the Mandan Indian village called On-A-Slant. On-A-Slant was a large village, occupied by the relatively peaceful farming people from about 1575 until 1781. At the end of the village's life, approximately 10,000 people lived there, raising corn, beans, and squash in the river bottoms of the Missouri and Heart Rivers.

Then catastrophe struck, in the form of small-pox infected blankets shipped upstream from American troops in St. Louis, Missouri. An estimated eighty percent of the village population died, and the survivors decided to move upstream, closer to the three Hidatsa villages located there. The Mandan had a loose friendship with the Hidatsa, and bought white trade goods from them, goods the Hidatsa obtained from British fur traders in Canada and their Assiniboine allies. The Mandan hoped that proximity to the Hidatsa would protect them from raids by their traditional enemies, the Arikara (ironically, now sharing a reservation with them) and the Yanktonai Dakota, among others.

Abandoned, the earth lodges that were the homes of the Mandan collapsed into themselves. The ditches built for protection gradually filled in, and the peeled cottonwood trunk palisade that had once surrounded the village rotted and vanished. Today, only ghosts inhabit the village.

At least, only ghosts are there during the night. During the long summer days, tourists are led through five of the six earth lodges built in the Civilian Conservation Corps days, under the instructions of Blue Corn Woman, the last corn priest and the first and only woman corn priest. (One of the lodges is closed because it's become unstable.) Traditionally, the earth lodges were built by women, who also did the farming. Men hunted, went on raids to steal horses and trade goods, and protected the village. One of the reconstructed lodges is the ceremonial lodge, a very large lodge that contains benches on which tourists can sit and listen to their guides, and where evening firelit talks are sometimes held.

Many visitors to On-A-Slant say that there is a feeling of something very old there. Some of the staff say that at night, you can be inside an earth lodge and hear voices, but when you step outside, no one is there. Sometimes you can hear music – not modern music, but flutes and drums. Some visitors claim to hear whispers. And staff says that after they leave the village, and know there's no one there, they sometimes hear a banging noise on the metal doors that close off lodges that need stabilization.

The large ceremonial lodge is home to the greatest sense of the past. Tour guides say that when they're inside, speaking, there's a sense that the audience is much bigger than the tourists that they can see. They remember that this was home to the Mandan for over 200 years, and the ceremonial lodge is a sacred place.

One story that may well be true concerns a former volunteer at the village. The grandmother of the Fort Lincoln Foundation's Development Director, Matt Schanandore, herself part Mandan, guided groups through On-A-Slant until her death. Since then, many visitors report that they have seen, and in some cases been guided by, an unknown woman without the recognizable tee shirt worn by Park employees. The description of this woman sounds a lot like Matt's grandmother. He acknowledges that she felt such a strong tie to the village that her spirit might linger, protecting the place she loves and greeting visitors with the traditional hospitality of the Mandan people.

In August of 2009, Dakota Paranormal Investigations (DPI) from Fargo did an investigation of the village. While they didn't catch anything paranormal on their video, and can't be certain that the muted voices they caught on audio tape weren't coming from the nearby campground, at least one of the crew had a personal experience, when something struck her on the back. Although DPI isn't positive it wasn't a bat – they're common in the village at night – they can't say for sure what it was. And it was a creepy evening.

On-A-Slant's Ceremonial Lodge, Ft. Abraham State Park, Mandan.

Killdeer Battlefield State Historic Site and Killdeer Medicine Hole
Killdeer

In the rolling country just east of the Badlands in southwestern North Dakota are the Killdeer Mountains, a beautiful range of hills covered with birch, beech, and oak trees. The mountains are rich with game, including deer, antelope, and game birds, and in fact their Dakota name meant "the place where we kill deer."

This was the place where General Alfred Sully fought a band of Dakota in 1864, as revenge for the Minnesota Massacre (an all-out attack by Minnesota Sioux on settlers and forts in 1862, angry over a treaty that gave most of their land to the Chippewa which was then ignored by white settlers; it led to them fleeing from Minnesota ahead of white forces, and ultimately was the catalyst for the "Indian Wars" that ended with the beginning of the reservation era). Sully had attacked a native village at Whitestone Hill in Dakota Territory in 1863, the bloodiest conflict ever held in Dakota up until then, but that wasn't enough for him.

In 1864, Sully led his forces into Dakota Territory again. Sully force-marched his men forty-seven miles on July 27th to get them within fighting distance of the Dakota. The Dakota scouts saw them coming, and, after concentrating the village on the Knife River, moved them to the base of the Killdeer Mountains, just south of the Badlands. The Dakota had somewhere between 3,000 and 5,000 warriors.

Sully thought the territory was too broken to fight on horseback, so he ordered his men to dismount. The Dakota warriors stayed on their ponies, watching in small groups on hilltops and ridges as the military force advanced. A Hunkpapa warrior named Lone Dog started the fight. He rode towards the soldiers, and when they fired at him, he rode back while his little group opened fire. The fight continued in this way, with little skirmishes as small groups of Dakota approached the troops then rode away, but the fight was moving closer and closer to the village.

The Dakota weren't able to stop or even slow the advance of Sully's troops. They had never encountered so many guns, much less the cannon that was used whenever they came into range. Eventually, they were involved in a fierce hand-to-hand combat in the brush and up the side of a steep butte. They finally broke and ran.

Sully won the fight, and the men, women and children of the Dakota scattered into the mountains. The women had managed to take down some of their skin lodges, and hide meat in ravines hoping to come back for it later, but Sully's troops destroyed everything they found, over 200 tons of food, clothing, and equipment. Before they left the next day, they also set fire to the woods in all directions.

The story of the Medicine Hole tells of a single band of Dakota, surrounded on a hill top, that suddenly disappeared. Sully's men searched, but couldn't find them. Hardly a week later, when Sully's men were searching the Badlands west of the Killdeer Mountains for any warriors who had escaped the battle, he came upon the same band of Dakota. In the story, the Dakota had gone through a small hole from the hill top, then through a series of tunnels and caves that brought them out in the Badlands.

You can visit the Medicine Hole yourself; it's a short walk from a small campground off Highway 22, north of Killdeer. The trail is marked. It leads you to the top of the hill, a place of strange rock formations and beautiful views. The Medicine Hole opening is large enough for a person to drop into it, but for years people have been dropping rocks into it. It has also been dynamited twice, once to close it, then again to open it again. About fifty years ago, a group of cavers managed to go about 175 feet down the hole. At that point they found three openings, all plugged with rocks. Through one opening, they could feel the movement of incoming wind.

After all the rocks and the dynamiting, you probably can't get down even a few feet now. But it's still worth visiting, and wondering what really happened there back in 1864. The Killdeer Mountains are keeping the secret to themselves.

Writing Rock

Near Grenora

In northwest North Dakota, about fifteen miles north and east of the small town of Grenora, are two granite boulders carved with petro-glyphs. This spot is called Writing Rock State Historic Site. Both rocks, a larger and a smaller boulder, bear the outline of the Thunderbird, a being sacred to the Late Prehistoric Plains Indian, regardless of nation. The Thunderbirds are inscribed with their wings outstretched, and are surrounded by what appear to be abstract designs. Although it's nearly impossible to date petroglyphs, and there are no datable artifacts with these boulders, archeologists know that the Thunderbird is very old. It has been found on bone jewelry, pottery, and even shells, dating from between A.D. 100 and A.D.1500. There are other sites within a 400 mile radius of Writing Rock that have similar petroglyphs.

Archeologists also say that the meaning of the Thunderbird is unknown. But the Brulé Sioux medicine man, John (Fire) Lame Deer told a story about them. The *Wakinyan Tanka*, the great thunderbird, once lived in a tipi in the highest peak in the Black Hills, but he doesn't live there anymore—too many white people! There are four old giant thunderbirds. The largest and greatest of these is the Thunderbird of the West. He wears clouds, and has enormous claws and big pointy teeth. His color is black. The second Thunderbird, from the North, is red. The third, from the East, is yellow, and the fourth, from the South, is white, but some people say his color is blue. That one has no eyes or ears, yet he can see and hear.

None of the People has ever seen a whole Thunderbird, only glimpsed pieces of them, so the People only know what they look like by putting all the pieces together. Sometimes they come and frighten those on a vision quest, but they aren't bad, they are good spirits. They like to help, but they may test you. Their symbol is a zig-zag of lightning with forked ends.

Long ago, there was another great being, but this one was a snaky water monster with feet and a big horn coming from her head. Unlike the Thunderbirds, the water monster hated people, and saw them as lice upon the earth's skin. She could make any river, even the Missouri, overflow, so she and all the little water monsters made all the rivers, creeks, lakes, and ponds overflow to kill all the people. Almost all of the people died, and only a few found refuge on the highest peak, and from there, they called to the great Thunderbirds to help.

The Thunderbirds heard them, and the Thunderbird from the West decided that they should help them, because they liked humans, and felt that they must have some purpose on earth. So they started to fight the water monsters. The battle was very fierce and went on for many, many years, with water everywhere and night seeming like day with the flashes of lightning. The great Thunderbirds used their claws and their big teeth to fight, while the water monster used her horn and the spikes on the end of her tail. The little thunderbirds fought against the little water monsters.

Finally the great Thunderbirds realized that the water monsters were winning. They flew to the top of the highest mountain to decide on a strategy. The greatest Thunderbird said that since their country was the air, and their power came from the sky, they had been foolish to fight the water monsters on the ground. They realized that they should use their thunderbolts instead.

So the greatest Thunderbird gave the word, and they all threw their thunderbolts together. All the forests started to burn, and the water began to boil. Soon the water was gone, and all the water monsters were dead. Since that was so, the great Thunderbirds claimed the power of water for their own. The people praised the great Thunderbirds and thanked them, and climbed down from the high mountain. The great Thunderbirds filled the rivers and lakes with new water, and the people repopulated the earth, and everything was good again.

It seems that the thunderbirds carved into the Writing Rock boulders may represent something after all, even if the archeologists don't believe stories.

Medicine Wheel
Northwestern North Dakota

Around 1900, Americans of European ancestry found a huge ring of rocks in the Bighorn Mountains. In the exact center of the ring was a cairn, and spoke-like rock lines went from the cairn to the ring. Knowing it had been made by the nomadic peoples of the plains, but not knowing its purpose, they called it a Medicine Wheel, and that name is still used by archeologists. The original number of the rings existing in the northern plains before the incursion of European Americans can't even be guessed at, but by looking at the destruction of tipi rings, smaller stone rings believed to have held down skin lodges, during the last 100 years, the number was probably enormous. Now, after years of vandalism, farming, and theft, only about 170 remain in the northern plains of the U.S. and Canada.

These medicine wheels are sacred to all of the Plains Indian people, but cultural anthropologists studying them have found that the meanings, purpose, and symbolism of the wheels are different for each tribe. Archeologist Ernie Walker of the University of Saskatchewan in Saskatoon says that most archaeologists identify eight different categories or styles of medicine wheels. Ian Brace, an archaeologist with the Royal Saskatchewan Museum in Regina groups them into only four categories: burial, surrogate burial, fertility symbols, and "medicine hunting."

Burial and surrogate burials are just what their names imply: graves and memorial sites. Perhaps the most recent medicine wheel known was built in 1938 to commemorate a great Blackfoot leader in Alberta, Canada. Fertility wheels are made to increase the fertility of the game a people hunted. When a group moved into a new area, they would build a ring and include buried gifts or offerings intended to increase the numbers of buffalo or other game. Patterns similar to those seen in fertility wheels, like radiating lines and circles, have also been found on birch bark "bitings" and pottery among artifacts from other pre-historic Native American peoples. These patterns were used for game animal fertility into early historic periods, so their purpose is known.

The "medicine hunting" category, which includes the largest surviving medicine wheel, the Moose Mountain Medicine Wheel in Saskatchewan, were used originally by burning bones, like shoulder blades, of the game on each line; when the bones cracked, sometimes globs of fat would come out, indicating that the line it was on pointed in a good hunting direction, and sometimes nothing came out, indicating a poor hunting direction. Brace thinks that over time these wheels were changed, and the remaining "spokes" provided a permanent hunting guide. That is, until Europeans arrived and moved or took the rocks. When the Moose Mountain Medicine Wheel was first seen by white people in Canada, in 1895, the center cairn was measured as being about 14 feet high. Today, it's only about a foot and a half, due primarily to theft of stones by those to whom the wheel is not sacred.

The earliest theory about medicine wheels is that they were calendars, the spokes pointing to the sunrise on equinoxes and solstices. This has been disproved, in part because it's impossible to see all the way across the larger wheels. The one at Moose Mountain, for example, is on a seventeen-foot-high ridge, and from one side of the ridge you can't see the other. The most obvious reason is that researchers who waited at a wheel for sunrises on those specific days found no correlation with the spokes. But regardless of the reason they were built, medicine wheels were sacred to the people who built them and remain sacred to their descendants.

So why is this discussion in this book? Because in northwestern North Dakota, somewhere "off the beaten path," is a medicine wheel, the only one known to still exist in the state. It has been recorded by the State Archeologist, and given a site number, but its location remains secret. Why? That should be obvious if you've read this far. Too many non-Native people who visit a medicine wheel feel the need to remove a rock and take it home as a souvenir, and if that continues, the wheel will vanish.

Although archeologists have dated the oldest wheels to over 4,000 years old, by dating materials left buried as offerings at the sites, most of the newer ones are no more than 800 years old, from the beginning of the time that the First Nations who made and know them came into the northern plains. The age of North Dakota's sole remaining ring isn't known.

If you want to see a medicine wheel, visit Medicine Wheel Park in Valley City, North Dakota. There, Valley City State University Professor Joe Stickler and his students have constructed a rock ring measuring 213 feet across. They built it as a calendrical ring, so the 28 spokes of the wheel represent the days in one lunar cycle. Six spokes extend beyond the wheel, and are aligned to show the position of the sun on the horizon at sunsets and sunrises on equinoxes and solstices. Stickler based the design on the Big Horn Medicine Wheel in Wyoming. Although most recognized prehistoric rings are not calendrical, it's certainly not impossible that some were.

The park also contains a model of the solar system, nature trails, a perennial flower garden, and an astronomy observation site. Also included is a section of the North Country National Scenic Trail (NCT), which when completed will be 4,600 miles long. It will reach from Lake Sakakawea in North Dakota to Crown Point, New York. Admission to the Medicine Wheel Park is free, but contributions for park maintenance are accepted.

Two Dakota Ghost Stories

In the stories that are told of ghosts among the Dakota and Lakota people, some are funny, some are a little creepy, and some make a good point. A funny story is "The Man Who Feared Nothing." It tells of four ghosts who hear about this fearless man, and decide to give him a good scare. They meet him one at a time, and he fears none of them, but succeeds in thoroughly scaring them. When he returns to his village to tell of his brave feat, a spider lands on his sleeve, and he quivers with terror until a little girl removes it. Not so brave then, was he?

"The Ghost Wife" is a Brulé story, about a man whose beautiful and beloved wife had already borne two children, then died giving birth to a third. The husband nearly went mad with grief; he cut off his little finger for her, held ceremonies for her, but nothing brought him peace of mind. One night he saw her ghost outside his lodge. She told him that she had seen him grieving and returned out of pity. They could all be together, she told him, if he would come with her to the place of spirits. Not being ready to die quite yet, he asked if she could come back and stay with them.

The ghost returned to the land of spirits to ask if that was possible. She returned with good news. If he would hang a buffalo robe and not even peek behind if for four days, then she would get her body back and could stay. Of course he did, and there she was, as lovely as the day she'd died. They lived happily for a very long time, but then the husband decided that he wanted more children and another wife. He married a pretty young girl. As often happens when a second wife enters the lodge, the new wife began to get more and more of his attention. The Ghost Wife was angry, but the new wife wasn't happy either. She told the first wife that she was nothing but an old ghost, and she should go away. The first wife said nothing, but when the new wife awoke the next morning, she was alone in the lodge. The Ghost Wife had taken her husband and children and gone to the spirit place, and now they would walk the Milky Way together, without the jealous new wife. The new wife was sorry for what she'd said and done, but the man, the first wife, and the children never returned from the spirit land.

The Roogaroo

Belcourt

Turtle Mountain Reservation

The word "roogaroo" comes from the French phrase *loup garou*, and means werewolf. It can be found in many places where there were French settlers or missionaries, including the bayous of Louisiana. But in Belcourt, the roogaroo comes from the Michif, or Métis. These are the mixed-blood descendants of French Canadian trappers and traders, and in most cases, Cree mothers. The Michif of the Turtle Mountain Reservation are enrolled members of the Turtle Mountain Band of Chippewa, their "cousins," but most came from Manitoba, Canada, after losing their land and property to the British Canadian government.

In Belcourt, the roogaroo isn't just a werewolf. It's a shape-shifting witch who usually takes on the shape of an enormous red-eyed black dog, and sometimes it's a devil man in a long black coat and hat, with glowing eyes, and sometimes a tail and cloven feet. It seems to depend on who is telling the story.

One roogaroo story I heard was about a couple in the 1920s who took their wagon from Belcourt one afternoon, along with another couple of friends, and went to visit the wife's sister and her husband in their cabin in the woods. Together they played cards for many hours, and drank chokecherry wine that the sister had made. They had a very good time, but the hours passed and it got dark, so they decided it was time to go home, because it was hard to play cards by lantern light, and they all had things to do the next day.

As they drove back through the woods, it was very dark. They couldn't even see the moon or stars because the branches of the trees made the road seem like a tunnel. Suddenly the horses stopped. The driver urged them to go, but they stood in place and shivered. He even used the whip, but they wouldn't move. His wife turned, and in the wagon behind them saw a giant black dog with glowing red eyes. She turned back quickly, and in a whisper, told the others that there was a roogaroo in the wagon, and he probably wanted to eat them. They all turned to look, and this time the black dog was right behind them, and they could feel his hot foul breath. "What shall we do?" cried the friend-wife.

"We must all say the Lord's Prayer, the Our Father," said the driver's wife, so they all did, and they said it three times. When they turned around, the roogaroo was gone, and the horses moved again and took them back into town.

Many of the people of Belcourt will tell you that the roogaroo is not just a story, and that he isn't just on the reservation. You can encounter him anywhere, and you'd better be sure you know what to do. It isn't just the older people who tell this, either. Many young people are just as strong in their belief.

Stones keep their secrets across the North Dakota prairie, and stories are still told around campfires and kitchen tables. Spirits roam the plains on the wind, and whisper to those who will listen. The cultures of the First Nations live on.

Bibliography

Books

Erdoes, Richard, and Alfonso Ortiz. *American Indian Myths and Legends.* New York, New York. Pantheon Books, 1984.

Hulse, Dean. *Westhope.* Minneapolis, Minnesota. University of Minnesota Press, 2009.

Jackson, William. *The Best of Dakota Mysteries and Oddities.* Dickinson, North Dakota. Valley Star Books, 2003.

_____. *Almanac of North Dakota Mysteries and Oddities, 2007-2008.* Dickinson, North Dakota. Valley Star books, 2006.

Langemo, Cathy A. *Images of America: Bismarck, North Dakota.* Chicago, Illinois. Arcadia Publishing, 2002.

Marsh Montana History Book Committee. *Marsh, Montana: Remembering the Yesteryears, 1910-1997.* Marsh, Montana. Self Published. 1998.

Norman, Michael and Beth Scott. *Haunted America.* New York, New York. TOR, 1994, 2007.

Ogden, Tom. *The Complete Idiot's Guide to Ghosts & Hauntings.* Indianapolis, Indiana. Alpha, 2004 (2nd Edition).

Terry, Maury. *The Ultimate Evil.* New York, New York. Barnes & Noble Books, 1987, 1999.

Thompson, Mike. *The Travels and Tribulations of Theodore Roosevelt's Cabin.* San Angelo, Texas. Laughing Horse Enterprises, 2004.

Periodicals

Albrecht, Mike. "Children of missing Hettinger couple ask for help." *Bismarck Tribune.* August 24, 2004.

Cook, Fred J. "Devil's Sex Slave." *True Police Yearbook*, vol. 7, 1956.

Domaskin, Andrea. "Family of missing Hettinger couple ask for public's help." *Bismarck Tribune.* August 8, 2004.

Donovan, Lauren. "Search widens for missing elderly couple." *Bismarck Tribune.* August 19, 2004.

Grantier, Virgina. "Missing couple's car found." *Bismarck Tribune.* November 5, 2004.

Gross, Glenore Larson. "Home spirit: House has a 'presence' near Bottineau." *Lake Metigoshe Mirror.* December 10, 2008.

Herzog, Karen. "Lakota: a language with its own spiritual message." *Bismarck Tribune.* May 12, 2005.

Kincaid, Sara. "The next generation in the study of Custer's Last Stand." *Bismarck Tribune.* November 18, 2007.

Spilde, Tony. "Yvonne Olson's body identified." *Bismarck Tribune.* November 9, 2004.

Woodward, Curt. "One worker killed, three injured in Four Bears bridge accident." *Bismarck Tribune.* December 1, 2004.

no byline. "Does victim of 1931 murder haunt library in Fargo?" *Fargo Forum.* October 20, 2009.

no byline. "Seven dead bodies found by Turtle Lake farmer." *Bismarck Tribune,* April 24, 1920.

no byline. "Hounds Trail Murderers." *Bismarck Tribune.* April 26, 1920.

no byline. "Sole Survivor of the Wolf Family, Foully Murdered Thursday." *Bismarck Tribune.* April 28, 1920.

no byline. "Authorities no closer to solution of Wolf murder; funeral of victims today." *Bismarck Tribune.* April 28, 1920.

no byline. "Arrests may be made today in murder case." *Bismarck Tribune.* April 29, 1920.

no byline. "Authorities to offer big sum for murderers." *Bismarck Tribune.* April 30, 1920.

no byline. "Murder suspect to be arrested in a day or two." *Bismarck Tribune.* May 11, 1920.

no byline. "Jacob Wolf, wife, 5 children and chore-boy murdered." *Turtle Lake Wave,* April 30, 1920.

no byline. "Henry Layer's confession." *Turtle Lake Wave,* May 21, 1920.

no byline. "Henry Layer, family slayer, dies in prison." Washburn Leader. March 22, 1925.

no byline. "Krem pastor slays maid, burns body; gets life term in prison." *Bismarck Tribune,* August 19, 1938

_____. "Remains found near Hettinger." *Bismarck Tribune.* November 6, 2004.

_____. "Guard joins in weekend search." *Bismarck Tribune.* November 13, 2004.

_____. "Horse riders join search." *Bismarck Tribune.* November 18, 2004.

_____. "Second body found in house." *Bismarck Tribune.* November 25, 2004.

_____. "No leads on missing area couple." *Bismarck Tribune.* August 21, 2004.

_____. "The things that go 'scrape' in the night." *Bismarck Tribune.* September 16, 2004.

_____."First lady visits North Dakota." *Bismarck Tribune.* October 2, 2008.

Other Resources

Thoreson, Joel, Chief Archivist, Evangelical Lutheran Church in America, correspondence.

http://www.aghost.us/106-VC.html

http://www.strangeusa.com

http://www.theshadowlands.net/places/northdakota.htm

http://www.ghostsofamerica.com/states/nd/html

http://samslovick.com/2009/10/16/statement-from-chief-arvol-looking-horse-regarding-sedona-sweat-lodge-deaths/

http://www.ndcourts.com/court/opinions/764.htm

http://www.prairieplaces.org/sims.cfm

http://www.byways.org/explore/byways/places/57506/index.html

http://www.killdeer.com/index.asp?Type=B_BASIC&SEC=%7B4B7F26F1-0479-4420-82F5-A2276E595141%7D

http://www.virtualsk.com/current_issue/endangered_stones.html

State Historical Society of North Dakota, pamphlets on State Historic Sites: Former Governor's Mansion; De Mores; Chateau de Mores; Writing Rock

Index of Place Names